LIFE
ACCORDING TO
MAAS ROY

WITHDRAWN

By Yvonne Archer
with
Stanley Roy Archer
August 2009

Archer Publishing 2009

D1493945

Cover Design: Carol Crosby

Illustrator: Jermaine Findlator

Editors: Yvonne Archer, Stanley Roy Archer

Copyright: © Archer Publishing 2009

Website: www.ourpeaceofhistory.com

E-mail: ourpeaceofhistory@gmail.com

Printer: Argun Printers, London

Published by © Archer Publishing 2009, the first from
the "*Our Peace of History*" series.

Warning:

A *few appearances of the colloquial words for faeces
and urine are contained in the text.*

CONTENTS

[Archer Publishing 2009]

ACKNOWLEDGEMENTS

Dad has always had a vision or perhaps a wish that I would someday become a writer although he's never explained why. And he passionately believes that I should write about my own life as soon as I'm able. Naturally, I've always seen dad as an amazing story teller and perhaps more importantly, a man of vision. So, this work has been developed within a framework of mutual love and respect.

As well as being immeasurably grateful for having played such a significant role in each other's lives, dad and I also wish to thank several other people who became invaluable to the realisation of these memoirs - in particular:

- ✓ *All the people from 'back home', their children, friends, neighbours from the Windsor Road area and Grafton School - for believing in our dreams and helping us survive the most difficult years, especially Aunt Ruby and Mr & Mrs Parish*
- ✓ *Ngozi Okwudili-Ince - for her immediate curiosity and recognition of the historic value of this story*

[Archer Publishing 2009]

- ✓ *Dave Neita - poet and 'people's lawyer' whose contagious enthusiasm, practical suggestions, feedback, advice, prayers and total belief in these memoirs provided fuel - plus our very first order based on the strength of a single draft chapter*
- ✓ *Carol Crosby, graphic designer and singer - for her creativity and considered practical advice*
- ✓ *Aunt Zillah - for her colourful contributions and encouragement*
- ✓ *Carol Malcolm, childhood friend - for strength, patience, encouragement, feedback and practical help through one of the most challenging times in her life; we fondly remember her brother Leslie as we leaf through these pages*
- ✓ *Christine Bramble, school friend - for her sincere interest and practical and literary suggestions*
- ✓ *Donovan Gauntlett - for safely transporting our priceless archive photos from Jeffrey Town, Jamaica to Miami - and then across the Atlantic to London*
- ✓ *Barry and Michelle of the Neunie clan for patient and consistent technical and moral support*
- ✓ *Kwame McPherson for generously sharing crucial details on the nitty gritty of self-publishing*

- ✓ *Uncle Isby for being the person who enabled us to print this book*
- ✓ *Jermaine, Yvonne's godson - for his enthusiasm, hard work, membership, the illustrations from his soul and his belief in the power of this project*
- ✓ *William Kremer, BBC colleague and friend - the Photoshop Wizard who always stepped in to save the day*
- ✓ *Jonathan Lewis of Argun Printers for his patience and hard work on his day off to help create a truly polished product*
- ✓ *The British Council's "Interaction: Trust the Difference" Leadership Programme and delegates from across Africa and the UK for encouraging us to take my Breakthrough Initiative,"**Our Peace of History**", from concept through to reality.*

Of course, we acknowledge that we are not solely responsible for our deeds and consciousness, and we continue to give thanks to a higher being for providing daily strength, constant love and guidance.

[Archer Publishing 2009]

Foreword

Between 1955 and 1959, 371 British Servicemen lost their lives during the 'Cyprus Emergency' leading to Cyprus' independence in 1960. This number includes 28 members of the Royal Navy and Royal Marines, 69 from the Royal Air Force and a staggering 274 from the British Army [ref 1 page 184]

To mark the 50th anniversary of the end of this bloody conflict, a memorial plaque will be unveiled in the old British Cemetery at Kyrenia on Remembrance Day, November 2009. This is being organised by David Carter and colleagues with the "full moral support" of The British Legion [ref 2 page 184]. We offer these memoirs as a contribution to help mark this event, to give a fuller historical vista and hopefully to serve as an historical and educational resource which specifically addresses the intertwined history of Britain and Jamaica.

It is our aim to ensure that these memoirs are included in the large body of works found in places like The British Library, The Imperial War Museum, the library of the

University of the West Indies, School for Oriental and African Studies and of course, local and school libraries across the UK and abroad. In fact, we believe that this type of material will be invaluable in raising the self-esteem of people of African descent, particularly our youths.

By providing a broader picture of the Black British experience, we believe we're starting a movement which will involve young people working with elders to also create literature, film, music, art, drama, photography etc. to also tell their stories. After all, <u>we</u> must be the ones to tell our own stories.

We've called our movement "*Our Peace of History*" because it aims to help push along the vital process of identifying and recognising Black people's contributions to British society as well as acknowledging the Black heroes walking tall amongst us. After all, they won't be around forever! And because of our own inter-generational experiences through writing these memoirs, we remain confident that by simply taking part in this creative process, peace and understanding amongst youths and elders will be promoted.

[Archer Publishing 2009]

We're sure that everyone involved will gain a renewed lease on life; there will be a fresh, vibrant, positive energy around Black people re-engaging with their history.

"*Our Peace of History*" has valuable lessons for us all to learn from, whatever our heritage and by being a part of this movement, we fully expect an immeasurable increase in confidence and self-esteem amongst both young and old. It is crucial that we openly and honestly re-examine our past without further delay so that we come to understand, acknowledge and celebrate the true worth of our elders whilst they're still amongst us - and make use of those old-time values they 'needs must' pass on.

This is an amazing moment in time for us all!

CHAPTER ONE
"The Intrepid Traveller"
The Mother Country calls her children

PART I

On October 13th 1954, Stanley Roy Archer made his way to a pier on Kingston Wharf in Jamaica. He had left his rural home in Jeffrey Town in the parish of St Mary and was living in Kingston Gardens near to Jamaica's famous Sabina Park Cricket Grounds and close to Mrs Manley's Art College. In his small brown leather suitcase, Stanley Roy carried the warmest clothing he was able to get his hands on as well as some pretty, colourful floral shirts which were in fashion at the time.

The one-way ticket for the voyage to England had cost Stanley Roy £75. Of course, that was in English money as Jamaica was a British colony at the time - so the island was owned and ruled by the British. His older brother Desmond (Dessie) had given him a loan to help him with the cost of the ticket –

"Which I paid back as quick as I could." Stanley Roy is quick to add.

[Archer Publishing 2009]

As he explained, such tickets were constantly being advertised in the newspapers and on the radio...

"They were very red hot at the time – the different voyages, different ships, different fares. About 3 or 4 ships kept coming around and they also called into other islands to take people to England.

It wasn't long after the war, so Europe was in one of the depressions and England needed people to help rebuild the country. We were cheap labour at the time and there were plenty of us and plenty work."

And so it was that Stanley Roy Archer heeded the call of the Mother Country – England.

There was quite a build-up leading to the big day when all his older brothers - Neville, Cecil, Dessie (Desmond) and some other friends accompanied Stanley Roy down to the wharf to see him off...

"Every afternoon for 8 days straight right up until the 13th of October, we had parties. There was drinking, ice-cream, cooking, friends and relatives! My parents didn't come – they were in country and in those days, life didn't allow it."

Travelling to the city of Kingston was not a simple matter for people in those days, unless they had a bicycle like Stanley Roy <u>and</u> were fit enough to ride there and back in a day. And all this was often done in the name of a good dance! Most people's lives were simply lead by the needs of family, land and animals so we can only imagine how Stanley Roy's poor mother and father must have felt at not being able to see young 'Sir Roy', as he'd always been called, before he set off on his long voyage.

The young Stanley Roy before he left Jamaica with his treasured bicycle

[Archer Publishing 2009]

Of course, back then, there was no telephone, letters took weeks to arrive by ship and even telegrams didn't arrive in the country overnight. So Elmore and Jeremiah Archer had absolutely no idea when they would see or hear from their son again; he'd planned to go away for about 20 years, get rich – and, he also wanted to get to Canada.

Stanley Roy had booked his ticket together with Tom, the brother of his friend, Clifford Ricketts. Uncle Clifford joined them later and was to become my Godfather.

> *"I was the first of my family and friends to leave, so it was big excitement! It was the first time I'd been on or inside a vessel, so I was excited. The only odd thing was not knowing the difference between 'dormitory class' and 'cabin class'; I didn't realise the difference until years on."*

There were plenty of bunk beds in dormitory class where Stanley Roy was booked on the MV Napoli and he quickly got to know everyone on the Italian vessel, both men and women - although the women were in their own cabins.

"We assembled on the sea deck and we had sports and games and so on. The ship picked up in Jamaica first so everyone in my dorm was from Jamaica."

But this refurbished war ship wasn't taking a direct route to the Mother Country, as Stanley Roy soon found out:

"On the way to London, we stopped in many places to pick up people on other Caribbean islands. And in Europe, we stopped in the Canary Islands, other parts of Spain and finally Genoa in Italy. And every time the ship stopped, we got a pass and went ashore."

And was that exciting?

"Well yes, it was something new; I always wanted to travel, so I was very excited."

Six weeks after he'd left Jamaica, Stanley Roy's sea voyage was finally over – well almost, as he explains further:

"If my memory serves me right, we disembarked on a Saturday in Genoa and got on a train. All night we travelled through the mountains and ended up in Paris on the Sunday morning where we had breakfast and we were allowed to walk around.

[Archer Publishing 2009]

They always had African people in Paris – they always had Africans there – so people didn't find us strange. We went to look at the Eiffel Tower and looked around. We were told what time to come back because we had to get to the station and get a train from Paris to Calais which was some miles away. We had lunch on the train to Calais before we got off and then we caught a ferry from Calais to Dover in England.

When we disembarked, we got a train from Dover to one of the main London stations. I can't remember whether it was Paddington or where. But it was evening when we arrived in London, so it was getting dark because it was winter.

I was personally excited because it was an adventurous trip. I didn't look back - I didn't think about things because when you're young, you can stand a lot of things; I didn't feel the cold yet!

But one thing that really astonished me was to see a white man sweeping up the train station. And even further surprising coming out of the station, was to see them sweeping the streets – because white men in Jamaica never did that!

Anyway, I joined with Tom and took a taxi. He was going to Brockley in South East London and I was going to Nelson Road in Hornsey, North London. The taxi man dropped me off first and he went and rang the doorbell – because we didn't know anything about doorbells - and Roy Hughes came down. He and the landlord were expecting me.

The house looked strange; there were narrow little stairs going up. Everything was shut up - doors and windows - and the lights were on all the time. I was to bunk down with Roy in his room but we didn't have long together as he went off to night work at a glass works – a foundry in Edmonton.

That was a Sunday, I remember. I listened to the radio for a little bit, I pulled back the curtain but I couldn't see anything much. You have to understand, that was before the Clean Air Act* so there were a lot of chimney pots. People burned coal, threw pieces of wood into the fire, anything – so it was smoggy.

[Archer Publishing 2009]

Everything was a bomb-site, a shambles when I arrived – very bad living conditions, things like that.

I remember one night when I was living in Hornsey, about early 1955, there was so much smog that many people couldn't find their street or their house and they got lost. Some people had to abandon their vehicles anywhere, even across the road. There was a blind white man in the area and he was the only one who could take us home because he didn't need any light to see. He was very popular!

Anyway, that first night, I went to bed and slept on and off in the strange surroundings. But I was awake when Roy Hughes got home early on the Monday morning, around or just after 7am. I looked through the window and saw all the chimneys giving out smoke. So I said: "What a lot of kitchen they have here, man!" And he said: "Man, a nuh kitchen - ah fire they have to warm up the place!" And he showed me the fire and how it worked.

There was no paraffin, kerosin oil or central heating or anything. Each house had 4, 5 or even 6 chimney pots because most of the rooms in the houses had a fire place. And of course, hot water bottles were very popular to warm up the bed before you got in."

Dad asked whether I remembered hot water bottles and I assured him that I did. Made of rubber, they were filled up with hot water from a kettle and then placed in your bed to warm it up during the cold nights. Despite numerous warnings, I'd often try to warm up my toes on my hot water bottle when I got into bed - and burn myself. This, of course, lead to itchy, unbearable 'chill blanes' in the winter - but the worst disaster had to be when your hot water bottle sprung a serious leak!

Anyway, what did Stanley Roy think of the food?

"As I found out, the food was mainly spuds – Irish potatoes - and rice pudding. And there was semolina, which was nearly like cornmeal porridge**, so I liked that. There was plenty of bread with bacon, sausages and eggs. But fish and chips was not my calling - nor the way it was being served in newspaper - which wasn't that nice when you look back at it now!

[Archer Publishing 2009]

The other thing was the unwrapped bread. They would leave it on the doorstep! And a lot of (Black) women used to go the bakers and get into fights. And many a time they would use their umbrellas. All Zillah (his school friend) *go ah road and mash up new umbrella 'pon people!"*

But let's get back to that shared room in Nelson Road because as I was to find out, there was a story behind it…

"I didn't stay there very long because I got into trouble with the landlady so I had to try to move before the landlord got home! The landlord was a Jamaican who went into the Air Force and managed to buy the house when he returned to London.

Apparently, every Saturday, we were to empty the dustbins, clean the stairs, dust off the banisters, and clean the kitchen, toilets and the windows. Those were the conditions you had to live under when you were renting. But one Saturday, I got in from work and felt a bit fed up and hungry so I made some bacon, sausages and eggs with a small loaf of bread and a cup of tea. I was just having a good snack before I started the house chores.

The landlady came upstairs and knew very well that I'd just come in so the dustbins hadn't been emptied and the stove wasn't cleaned because I'd just finished cooking on it. The bins, cooker and sink were all on the landing – so she put the dustbin right in front of the room door. So I had to either step in it, step over it or remove the bin to get out the door.

I had on a very strong-bottomed pair of shoes which I'd made myself in Jamaica (one of Stanley Roy's numerous trades was shoemaking) *so I decided to give the bin a kick and it started to go down the stairs. And the rubbish went all the way down to the landing and messed up the place from top to bottom! So the woman wasn't very pleased and when my roommate came in; she complained to him before he got up the stairs.*

Roy Hughes said: "'Man, ah what dat you do?! We have to go look a room NOW!" So we cleaned up and went to the station in Finsbury Park where they used to display rooms for rent and bikes for sale etc. on the notice board.

That night, the landlord came upstairs. His wife had complained to him so he <u>had</u> to come. He came up very slowly, counting out each step on the way and humming a tune, checking for dust on the banister with his finger. Maybe he was trying to scare me! And when he got up the stairs, he started to talk saying things like: if it wasn't for them - the Air Force people who stayed on after the war - we who just came from Jamaica wouldn't have anywhere to stay.

And eventually, he came out with it - that he used to do boxing in the British Air Force as a way to threaten us, saying: "I'm a <u>pugilist</u>". I wasn't easy back then, so I look in his face, I look in his eyes and I said to him: "I'm not a boxer, but I'm a <u>butcher</u>". He took one look in my face and turn 'round and head <u>straight</u> back downstairs to his wife. That frightened the shit out of him.

In those times, I couldn't lose, even if he was a pugilist – in fact, I would've cut him out of his bloody clothes!"

So there ended Stanley Roy's stay in what has become the very trendy Hornsey, Crouch End area!

Luckily, two brothers (friends of Roy Hughes) were buying a place in Ashbrook Road, Archway, and Stanley Roy rented the attic. So that's where his friend Busha Bennett came when he arrived in 1955, then his brother Lucien Bennett followed by their cousin, Lowell (Mel) Sadler later on.

"Lowell came to his mother, Miss Ivy ('Big Granny') and we took the 17 trolley bus down to the Cale (Caledonian Road) to 4 Oldershaw Road to see her. Uncle Lucien eventually went off to Birmingham and Uncle Isby, Mel's brother, came down from Birmingham. We all ended up living in Oldershaw Road and then we moved to 50 Eburne Road in Holloway where many of you were born. That house was jointly owned by Busha, Isby and Lowell."

[Archer Publishing 2009]

And that's how people from our community made progress back in the early days; they shared rented rooms, worked together to put on fund-raising parties and worked any job to help each other buy the houses we grew up in. So we, as children, were privileged to grow up around our elders and as a result, had numerous 'aunties', uncles' and even 'grannies' – and thank goodness for people like Aunt Ruby, Little Granny and Big Granny!

1966 - Uncle Lowell aka Mel (left) and Uncle Isby outside 50 Eburne Road, a 3 floor terraced house which they'd bought along with their cousin Uncle Busha (Bennett)

But just as our elders were arriving in London, others like Roy Hughes and later on, Aunt Daphne and Aunt Dotty were leaving. Like several others, Roy Hughes had always been 'on his way to America' as it was easy to get there via England. As Stanley Roy explains it, following World War II, Winston Churchill who was Britain's Prime Minister at the time, had closed a loophole in the law which made it more difficult for Jamaican passport holders to take up the quota for American visas from Jamaica.

At that time, Jamaicans were British & Commonwealth Citizens and Churchill wanted them in England to work and help rebuild the Mother Country following her losses. But of course, the young Jamaicans soon found that it was fairly easy to get to America from England, so they began to use England as a stepping stone. After all, they simply wanted to get rich quick and they'd heard that The US of A was the place to do that!

NOTES

* The Clean Air Act came into effect from 1955 following the Great Smog of 1952, limiting the use of certain types of fuel which caused heavy air pollution.

** Cornmeal, also known as 'polenta' in some parts of the world, is a popular ingredient for porridge amongst Jamaicans.

[Archer Publishing 2009]

School friend Aunt Zillah with chief bridesmaid **Olive Malcolm** (Photo courtesy of Olive)

PART II

Stanley Roy had also answered the Mother Country's call because he too saw it as an opportunity to get rich quick, although, as mentioned earlier, his original plan was to head out to Canada. But in the process, he became 'Ray' because in those days, no-one had ever heard the name 'Roy' before and they certainly couldn't pronounce it. Little did they know that 'Roy' meant 'King' – and that this very same Roy would later display the leadership qualities coveted by any true royal.

But let's get it straight: the reality was that the common Englishman wasn't about to put himself out for what he considered to be any bleeding 'posh' foreign name – or any foreigners for that matter. So the day after his arrival in England, Roy became 'Ray' in the hunt for a job!

> "*On the Monday, Roy Hughes took me to the Labour Exchange in Medina Road to register for work.*"

'The Labour Exchange' is now the Job Centre which dad was surprised to learn is now back on Medina Road in Finsbury Park…

> "*They recommended I go training for British Telecom. But you had to board out* and the money that they offered was less than what I was earning in Jamaica. So I couldn't accept that because I went to England to work, get rich quick and do what I want to do - look after my people, etc.*
>
> *My first job was in Barkingside at 'British Paints'. I worked 6 days a week but the money went on fares mainly. The foreman used to give me overtime mixing resin for making varnish along with another chap, Ron. But to my surprise, Ron couldn't read or write.*
> (We'll hear more of Ron later!)

[Archer Publishing 2009]

It was very, very far for me to leave from Hornsey to Barkingside and we went through the Blackwall Tunnel, part of the journey. The single decker 233 bus used to go up Ferme Park Road to Finsbury Park. From there, I used to get the 106 to Barkingside and then I had to pick up another bus through the Blackwall Tunnel to where I was going.

At that time, they had the Penny Haypenny** workman's ticket on the bus so if you got the bus before a certain time and got off by a certain time, you could get that cheap fare. But my journey was so far that before I got off the bus, they would come back to me to make up the fare.
My very first day of work was a Saturday and we only worked half-day so the fares and national insurance took everything I earned; I didn't get a penny out of it!

Fortunately, the foreman there said it's too far for me to come to work and every morning I was late. I couldn't leave any earlier from Hornsey. Every day he had to go and take the key to open the clock and clock me in. That's how lucky I was; he just took to me.

So he advised me to go back to The Labour Exchange and tell them my foreman said 'it's too far and it's getting cold'. Remember, it was winter when I got to London. He even gave me a gabardine rain Mac which he said he wasn't wearing, because I didn't have a coat.

So as advised by his foreman, Stanley Roy took the next Saturday off and returned to the Labour Exchange…

"They offered me a job at the Islington Borough Council Cleansing Department***. When I went back to work on the Monday, the foreman asked which department I'd been offered a job in, but I didn't know anything about that so he couldn't say whether I should take the job or not.

But anyway, he said the money and time it took me to get to Barkingside - it wasn't worth it. So I took the other job. I have to be thankful to him for putting me straight and for the use of his coat. I had it for quite some time.

[Archer Publishing 2009]

In Islington, I was on what you call 'the conveyor belt'. At that time, recycling was <u>big</u> business - so some people picked up metal, others clothing, some knives and forks when they went past on the conveyor belt.

Clothing was used to make rags for cleaning machines in industry etc, so they made money. But there was a lot of ash because of burning coal so it was a very dusty job - very dusty. Anyway, the rest was emptied out into railway cars which took the rest of the rubbish to dumping grounds out in the country.

During the war, a lot of house owners died and did not return to their residence - also shops, warehouses and so on. Their wives and children would be evacuated way up in the Midlands where they made the war ammunition at the factories; Coventry, Wolverhampton, Birmingham were all good places for hardware.

So 'dad' didn't come back from war, the families had been cleared out so the council had to get the

*houses ready for people to live in them again. And of
course, they would just dump what they found as there
was nobody to claim the stuff.*

*Trucks from the cleansing departments were sent to
clear out their premises and as the council would only
have dumped the stuff, the men came back with some
goodies. People used have things stored up and never
returned to claim their property and belongings.*
*We know a man whose second-hand furniture shop
was off the Caledonian Road and he told us on many
an occasion that he made his fortune by buying a
second-hand settee set. One of the chairs was packed
with money!*

*He was a very nice man – he was very friendly with
Black people. He might have been mixed-race but
where he was from was something he didn't discuss.
He would trust**** you furniture and he'd let you pay
him little, little.*

*Pawn Shops and Second Hand shops were big
business at the time, and even for us that worked
there* (at the cleansing department) *– I was fortunate*

[Archer Publishing 2009]

to get looked after every time. And it was always white men, English men on the trucks who always brought back things that they thought I'd need from these clear outs.

Once, they went to clear out a warehouse and they brought back about 3 large cartons of brand new shoes and boots. Of course, I was one of the beneficiaries. Although I didn't go out, whatever they got, they always shared with me. If they found money, which they normally did, they always gave me a share of it.

Next, I went on the buildings - steel bending and fixing. After that, I worked for London Transport Underground as a Station Man. Work was so plentiful that I could leave one job at 12 o'clock, have my lunch and start another one at 1 o'clock - because England was in the process of rebuilding.

During the recession following the long war, there was plenty of work. Skilled labour on the buildings was scarce so there were lots of jobs for me. Of course, I got a lot of jobs on the building for people when they first arrived in England. Once I worked there and told the foreman about them, they always said: 'bring them!'"

NOTES

* Some companies provided lodgings or a room and meals for trainees, deducting the cost from their wages.

** One and a half old British pennies – worth a fraction of a British penny today.

*** Where the Arsenal Emirates Stadium stands today

****'trust' was another term for 'credit' or 'getting things on tick' - where you were trusted to pay someone as arranged.

PART III

"I was shocked to find the clothes that English people were wearing were worse than what my mother used to put out as doormats to wipe our feet on before I left Jamaica.

Charcoal grey was very popular, also black and navy blue - and sometimes, the richer people or officials would wear pinstripes, trilby hats and detached collars. But I couldn't believe how poor people were in England.

[Archer Publishing 2009]

Pawn shops were a big thing in those days and that was something we weren't used to; we weren't used to that in our culture. Of course, what people used to do every week was put in the husband's one suit that they owned on say a Monday, and take it out on Friday when it was pay day."

When I told dad's school friend Aunt Zillah, that we were working together on writing these memoirs, she was really pleased and proud of us. After telling me several amusing stories of her own, Aunt Zillah quickly confirmed dad's account of the clothing owned by poorer English people 'in the old days':

"*Some of the people suit was <u>so</u> shine with dirt, you could have write yuh name on it with a hair pin*!" she said, by way of explaining how most English men at that time only owned one well-worn, unwashed suit. People like Stanley Roy and Aunt Zillah soon realised that they really hadn't been as poor as they'd thought back home in Jamaica.

And as for fashion – dad felt that he was well ahead of the game:

"It's only after West Indians came that English people started changing their style completely and wearing more clothes - and everyone started getting jealous.

Then the Italians came and the Greeks and they further influenced the fashion. Late night, early morning parties* - we started all that. We wore broad ties printed with women and colours etc.

I remember one day before I put on my overalls, when I was working at Pearl Insurance on the building work in Holborn, someone shouted out: 'Hey, Ray came to work in his pyjamas!' I had turned up to work in one of the pretty-pretty shirts I'd brought with me from Jamaica!"

But as Stanley Roy also recalls, not all his early experiences of London were quite as funny…

"Hells Angels and Teddy Boys** were around in those days so racial prejudice and non-acceptance, especially among men, became a trend.

Another thing I know of – a lot of the woman had Black men but when they were with other white people, they would become a double-edged sword because they had to keep up with them and talk against Black people whenever that was the talk. But I personally know of 2 women in the canteen at work who talked racism but went home to meet their Black boyfriends!

Black people had to defend themselves but people were afraid of Jamaicans. So Black people from other islands were less likely to be troubled if they said they were Jamaicans and tried to speak like Jamaicans. A lot of that used to go on."

NOTES

* Fondly referred to as 'blues' and 'shubeens', these parties went on into the early hours of the next morning. Party goers were charged for drinks and food and the money raised was often used as deposits on houses.

** White men and teenagers who could be easily identified by their clothes and hairstyles.

CHAPTER TWO

"The Solider"

The Mother Country calls some of her children, again

By 1956, Stanley Roy Archer, aged 22, had already been in England for 2 years. He was an old hand! As we've discovered, life in London wasn't perfect but the man was having fun. And as we've learned, some of Stanley Roy's childhood friends from back home had joined him, so life in north London became even better.

Never out of work, Stanley Roy had enough money to spend his Saturday nights in the West End, dancing to ballroom and jazz music with stunning women until the wee hours of a Sunday morning.

And Stanley Roy has always claimed that he and his friend Uncle Isby were usually the only two true jazz dancers at pubs in Turnpike Lane and basement clubs from Warren Street through to Piccadilly. Only they had the ability to let loose enough to really feel the music and let it dictate their moves. Perhaps this explains why, when it comes to dancing, I seem to have few genuine inhibitions?

Anyway, one day in the summer of 1956, someone knocked on the front door of 163 Caledonian Road, so Stanley Roy ran down the stairs and opened it to a suited, booted white man wearing a hat.

"*Stanley Roy Archer*?" the man asked in an official tone.

"*Yes?*" he answered truthfully; he was curious about what this white man could possibly want with him. He was sure the man wasn't a policeman because Stanley Roy had kept his nose Kleenex Clean since he'd arrived from Jamaica by ship in 1954.

And then it hit him with a force – or least, the palm of his hand hit his own forehead squarely with a SLAP! Damn – he'd just identified himself and had just been called up for National bloody Service!

It was the law – compulsory that every man of working age had to serve their country. And the boys from the West Indies who, shortly after World War II, had answered the call of the Mother Country to fill those vital job vacancies that the English didn't want to fill, weren't exempt. They'd been called to duty again.

These Black boys were definitely British for the purposes of National Service and neither Queen nor country gave two hoots that they were only in England to make money to send back home to help their families. Once they'd been in the mother country for two years, she called them again and expected them to give back much more than labour and taxes by doing at least two years of National Service.

Stanley Roy hadn't been thinking; the man had caught him on the hop – totally off guard. Everyone in the house knew that if any white men came to the door and asked for any of them by name, you were supposed to open up your eyes wide and look as helpful as possible when you said:

   "No governor, there's no-one here by that name. Sorry, can't help!"
And if you were feeling particularly brazen, you could add:

   "Have you tried next door, mate?"

Within two weeks of being identified, Stanley Roy's 'letter of posting' with a one-way train ticket had arrived. The letter informed him that he had a fortnight's notice to report in and that his job would keep his post open for him. If he ended up doing more than the minimum of 2 year's National Service, his job would be gone - but then the military would help him find a new one on his return.

> "*Government jobs, like work on the railways, would always take ex-National Service men as long as they were qualified for the post*", he recalls.

So Stanley Roy Archer had better 'pack his grip' and get ready for the unexpected - or maybe for what he'd heard about when he was still a growing lad back home in Jamaica.

Several Jamaican men had sustained injuries during World War II fighting for Britain in Europe and Stanley Roy remembers seeing them when they returned home. As he recalls:

> "*Seeing men who'd lost limbs or their sight was a common thing. They were just sent back to their villages without any assistance; I don't believe they*

*got any. They had to depend on relatives, those
who couldn't manage."*

And Stanley Roy went on to explain what life was like for
many of the ex-military men once they'd returned home
to Jamaica:

> *"They were able to do work on small holdings; they
> would cultivate plants and provide food for
> themselves. Others couldn't even maintain
> themselves so they lived by the generosity of family,
> children and other relatives.*
>
> *Some had to improvise to make artificial limbs for
> themselves by using tree trunks or limbs of trees. We
> spoke to them all the time and we would open our
> mouths wide when we spoke to them about foreign
> lands."*

For youngsters like Stanley Roy, those men who'd been
abroad during the war were amazing so they had
amazing tales to tell. My dad reminded me, with delight,
of the reaction he'd get from me and the friends I grew up
with as he told us about the country he came from…

[Archer Publishing 2009]

"It was like when you were small and I was telling you all about Jamaica and your mouths were open wide! You just laughed and imagined like it was a fairy land you were hearing about. You had no questions at all – only listened.

And it was the same when <u>we</u> were small; we didn't have any questions, even if it was lie they were telling! Some exaggerated their adventures to seem bigger than they were. They told us how they travelled on the ship on the open seas because there was no passenger plane as such. Planes came after World War II.

The men also talked about white people and white soldiers. They told us how it was two different worlds for Black and white. They talked of Germans and those were one of the people they <u>had</u> to know about.

Some who were fit did very well when they got home *and improved and had a different outlook on life. They walked and talked differently and stood up erect as soldiers. I didn't want to be in a war at all*

but I wanted to travel. I understood that I could be a
soldier and not go into war, but I could get travelling
out of it."

Unfortunately, it just so happened that when Stanley Roy
was forced to become a soldier himself, his opportunity to
travel also included going to war. A civil war was raging in
Cyprus so now the Mother Country had called him to duty
not once, but twice. And if necessary, she'd take his blood
too.

He was left to deliver the news to his bosses about being
called up for National Service. "*Oh dear, oh dear, oh dear,*"
was the type of reaction he got from his bosses on the
Underground, as they expressed their sympathy.

> "*We'd like to help you Ray - you know we'd rather*
> *keep you. You're a good worker, but you're just not*
> *exempt."*

They even allowed him to keep his special privilege pass for
British Rail and the Underground, even though he was
going away. And it was true about him being a good Station
Man but that still didn't make him exempt from National
Service.

[Archer Publishing 2009]

'Ray' had been working with London Transport for less than six months so his National Service could not be deferred.

At the time, when people like Stanley Roy were the backbone of London's transport system, England really needed its buses and trains to get as many people to work as possible - especially as so many of her workers had been killed during the Second World War. But England would simply have to find a way to run the country without Ray.

One thing Stanley Roy didn't expect to learn at a previous job was that his 'boss' – the senior man to him at 'British Paints' - wasn't eligible for National Service. And what a shock it turned out to be to when he discovered why! And that there were many other white people in the Mother Country who, like Ron, couldn't read or write.

> "*Ron was of no use to the army – not even National Service would tek im*", as Stanley Roy bluntly put it.

Although he'd left school at 14, Stanley Roy's Jamaican education turned out to be more than adequate for doing and even checking Ron's work at the paint factory.

Stanley Roy could accurately measure out resin and spirit for the paints and varnish using old-fashioned weights. And he could also write down the measurements as necessary in a neat, legible hand. How then could Ron be his senior – his boss? Why wasn't Stanley Roy promoted?

Once, while working in another job along Holloway Road, dad was offered a chance to take up a promotion but he refused the offer. He'd been working alone in his area and had a lovely fire near his workshop to keep him warm while he did nothing but wait for the machine to do its job.

It was during these waiting periods that the boss would come and talk to Stanley Roy to find out about Jamaica and exchange views and ideas. In addition, he'd often receive visits in his workshop from a Hungarian man who'd come to live in London. He'd use Stanley Roy, not the Englishmen, to improve his English and would do this by using a pocket dictionary with translations.

It was through this man that Stanley Roy found out more details on the Hungarian revolution of 1956; he was getting

[Archer Publishing 2009]

first-hand reports rather than just reading about it or listening to news reports on the radio. Stanley Roy soon realised that his workmate was very well educated and had been an official football referee back in Hungary. Unfortunately, he'd had to flee the country leaving behind his wife and children.

Anyway, dad was happy in his job and the promotion was offered to and accepted by another Black man. He was well qualified for the job and had worked there for some time. But with a new Black boss in place, several white men walked off the job and point blank refused to work under him - because of his colour.

Although things are not as blatant today, such issues have remained relevant to people who look like Stanley Roy, including me - his mirror image, right through to the 21st century.

CHAPTER THREE
"Solider and Student"
A 2nd chance for an education

Stanley Roy Archer became one of the intakes of late summer 1956 to 1957 and off he went to endure twelve weeks of square bashing. Yes, officially, twelve weeks of training was thought to be all that a young man needed to gain the necessary skills required to kill and die for his mother country. Just twelve weeks.

Young Stanley Roy took a train to Oswestry, Shropshire in the Midlands and as he waited at the train station for the truck, which transported soldiers to base camp, he spotted another Black man who said:

"I bet I know where you're going!"

"Where?" replied Stanley Roy.

"Oswestry – that's where I'm going too!" And the man was indeed correct; they were both off to do their National Service.

The man's accent easily identified him as a fellow Jamaican and during their general chit-chat, Stanley Roy found out that his fellow traveller had also been living in London. And as was the way, and still is with many Black people who've moved to a country where they've found that they're in the minority, the two men soon wanted to know more. Which part of Jamaica was the other man from? And they went on to share one other vital detail:

> *"It was a long time ago so I can't remember his name, but we had a chat about general things - and we both said how we really didn't want to do National Service and were missing Civvy Street and so on. It wasn't <u>our</u> choice to go - we were conscripts."*

So the new conscript, Stanley Roy Archer, soon became known as 'Dan Archer', even by the officers, because the name 'Archer' wasn't very common. Dan Archer was a famous character in the ever popular BBC Radio 4 programme "*The Archers*", which I made the mistake of classifying 'a soap opera'. But dad firmly asserts that it's much better than that – so we'll call it a drama about English farm life!

Anyway, over to the newly named 'Dan Archer':

*"When we got to base camp, we were in completely different groups but every night we used to meet up at the NAFA (*phonetic: Naff-A – the Navy, Air Force and Army canteen*). And we saw each other regularly as we went out to different places during training. Then later on, he told me that he had told them (the Army officials) that he couldn't read and write so that they would throw him out! Somebody had told him to tell them that."*

Remember Stanley Roy's boss, Ron?

During training, the men were taken to Wales on a camping trip where Dan Archer's impression of the area and the Welsh mountains was *"quite nice"'*. The hostile and mountainous landscape was *"perfect for training"* as he put it - but the Welsh landscape also held other surprises for the trainee soldier...

"When we were out there, I saw a Black man out in the heat of the hot sun. It was summer at the time and it was hot and the Black man was in the hills digging trenches bare-backed – no shirt! And I recognized him as the same Jamaican man.

[Archer Publishing 2009]

When we went back to camp, I looked for him in the NAFA. And when I caught up with him, we spoke 'naturally', you know quite a lot of blue language, as we used to in those days. And I said: '*&^^&! Man, I thought you were gone!' and he told me that they had put him into the engineering section where you didn't need to be able to read and write very well!

The section he was put into wasn't the Royal Engineers though, where they did mechanics on trucks etc. No, he was in the section where the engineers were responsible for digging trenches, laying telephone lines high up in trees and under the ground, fixing roads and so on. And they just had a few officers to tell them what to do. It was a lot of manual work - so his trick to get out of National Service didn't work at all!

Anyway, *I suspect they used to watch us to find out whether we could really read and write. Remember, the lads were young; they were homesick and were missing their mums and dads so they (*the army officials*) would watch to see who could read their own letters from home and who would write back".*

So of the three Black men that we know of, who was a part of the intake of 1956, it was only Dan Archer who was sent out to Cyprus - as far as we know…

"The very well educated man from St Vincent was probably sent to do administrative work in an office somewhere because he could read and write extremely well - but he didn't have the physical abilities to be an active soldier. Give him a book and he was fine. But the physical side of things, he just couldn't manage.

The Jamaican guy _did_ have the physical capabilities but there wasn't much call for trench digging and telephone lines out in Cyprus because it was mainly villages and farm land - small holdings."

But back to square bashing; what was everyday life like for Dan Archer? Well, it meant crack of dawn mornings, polishing of boots, making of bunks and ruddy-looking white men shouting at him all the time. So it quickly became apparent that square bashing was going to be no holiday.

However, rifle practise was *"fun"* – which probably explains why some years later, as his daughter, I always got any prize I'd set my heart on at the funfair if a shooting game was involved. Dad never missed!

But even as a little girl, I instinctively knew that the gypsies at the funfair, as we called travellers at the time, didn't like Stanley Roy, especially as his shooting skills were always spot on and they had to pay up with prizes. And I was never, ever allowed to have toy guns. I knew this had nothing to do with me being a girl, but it was many years before I really understood dad's reason.

Now the class on hygiene during square bashing was far from fun for Stanley Roy – in fact, it left him deeply offended. The intake was taught when to brush their teeth, how to use toothpaste and even how to position their wrists and move the toothbrush up and down to ensure that their teeth were brushed properly.

> *"I thought 'how dare they?!' Who did they think they were to instruct a big man on such matters? What type of home did they think I had come from?"*

At the tender age of 24, Stanley Roy was the oldest man in the group and yet he was the only one who could lay claim to the fact that he still had all his own pearly white teeth.

Back home in his district or 'village' of Jeffrey Town, St Mary, Sir Roy (as knighted by his elders) had grown up utilising a dental hygiene routine that would put modern-day orthodontists to shame.

Rather than a toothbrush and toothpaste, he'd use 'chew stick' – a natural alternative for both as it contained ingredients to clean and strengthen both teeth and gums. And studies would certainly show that the use of fluoride supplements in the water couldn't strengthen teeth or polish tooth enamel as effectively as chew stick.

And rather than dental floss, which wasn't yet in use, after eating stringy sugar cane or mangoes, there was nothing like a piece of thread to thoroughly clean between the teeth and massage the gums - strengthening them even further.

Many years later, we were to conclude that my father's age old methods of dental hygiene must have arrived in

[Archer Publishing 2009]

Jamaica with the Africans who had been enslaved. I can still remember dad's excitement when his Nigerian friend 'Doc' brought him back some particularly tough chew stick from Nigeria in West Africa. And the discovery that a Nigerian and a Jamaican shared the same basic method of brushing their teeth brought an additional closeness to their relationship. Doc's teeth, needless to say, were also perfect.

Doc – Dr Ephraim – had trained as an acupuncturist and homeopathic doctor in China at a time when it was unheard of for Africans to travel to China. His training took place during an era when ideas of natural therapies and holistic medicine were certainly thought of as ridiculous hocus-pocus by those practising traditional western medicine. But years later, doctors of Western medicine are still being forced to re-examine and rethink their ideas.

Anyway, the sense of outrage, injustice and deep offense at being given a dental hygiene lesson by the British Army back in 1956 were feelings that would remain with Stanley Roy during his lifetime. And more than 50 years after leaving the army, he still managed to work up a serious string of words to show how his utter outrage still burned strong…

> *"De amount of bridge, plate and false teet* (teeth) 'mongst dem was something to behold! And me was de only man there who did have 32 white, glistening, sound teet. Well, you know <u>my</u> teet! Now can you imagine what dem did look like inna 1956?!"*

And it was true. Dad's smile always drew automatic admiration – and seemingly made women weak at the knees – something I noticed from an early age. But, dad hadn't finished venting his spleen yet:

> *"And di damn man waan** come tell me how fi brush my teet?? Damn outta order!! Mi all go ah one Australian dentist in Seven Sisters Road, right there over McDonalds. You remember him?"*

I told him that I did, but that I'd thought the Dentist was a South African.

> *"No!"* dad corrected very firmly.

Remember, in those days, people like dad went to anti-apartheid protests and meetings with me in my pram - and boycotted goods from South Africa. So he might not have been so comfortable with a South African dentist. No, his dentist:

[Archer Publishing 2009]

"…was an Australian. Him used to marvel at the beauty of my teeth. I remember one time I did need a filling but I just tell him to tek out the bloody thing. Him couldn't get it out so him haffi*** send me to the dental hospital but dem couldn't get it out either.

In the end, he suggested a sledge hammer and it tek <u>6</u> ah dem to tek out de one teet! Dem cut de gum and de bone to get it out. And nothing was wrong with de teet. I suppose in those days, they never knew about root canal." (Ouch!)

And just to be sure that he'd got his point across about the hygiene class during square bashing – again – Stanley Roy added:

"And di damn man waan come tell <u>me</u> how fi brush my teet?! Damn outta order!!"

NOTES:

* teet – Jamaican patois for 'teeth'

** waan – Jamaican patois for 'wanted to'

*** haffi – Jamaican patois for 'had to'

1956 - Gunner Archer during square bashing at Kiwi Gordon Barracks in Bulford, Wiltshire

CHAPTER FOUR
"An Eager Schoolboy"
Education, Equality and Justice

So, as one of the oldest men in the 25th Field Regiment Royal Artillery, 24 year old Gunner Archer commanded more respect than most of the others - but for more reasons than just his age…

> *"Before I worked on London Transport, I was working as a steel bender so although I wasn't very tall, I was extremely muscular and stronger than most."*

And that physique certainly helped during his army training – although perhaps not in the obvious way. You see, Gunner Archer was one of only two Black men in the entire battalion.

As mentioned earlier, Gunner Archer had left school at 14 and later, would describe himself as *"semi-literate"* despite having worked in London with people like Ron. Now here, I'm forced to go off on a slight tangent to accommodate Stanley Roy's take on education. It's a tangent that will help us understand more about what shaped him as a confident, fearless, dignified man and soldier - despite the obstacles thrown in the paths of men who looked like him.

Two of his firmly held beliefs became:
1) the world is full of 'educated fools' and
2) it's full of people who use their education to exploit the uneducated.

Throughout the years, Stanley Roy has maintained that the teachers back home in Jamaica simply forced children to memorise facts rather than helped them to enjoy learning. He also maintains that most teachers shouldn't have been in the profession at all. And in his opinion, the brutal beatings that he and other children suffered at the hands of their teachers was the real reason why children tried to learn what was being taught. Fear and cruelty were the main lessons taught at Jeffrey Town Elementary School - as with most schools across Jamaica at the time.

But elementary schools took children from age 7 to 16 and taught all subjects. And those who stayed on until they were 16 took the Jamaica Local Examination, and if they passed, they were well equipped to go onto further education.

[Archer Publishing 2009]

But back to discipline; unfortunately, stories of beatings by teachers were confirmed by Aunt Zillah many decades later when she shared her memories of an horrific beating that my dad received one day. She remembered how Teacher S.W. Fagan - 'Shit Wet Fagan' to the children – would wear either a black or a white suit to school each day. And if he wore his black suit,

"*Watch out,*" Aunt Zillah said, "*because that meant he was in a bad mood - and there would be trouble!*"

As did all the teachers, S.W. Fagan had a belt which he'd given a special name – and it was used solely for beating children. So it was this special 'friend' of 'Shit Wet Fagan' that helped him to brutally meat out his own form of justice to little Stanley Roy one particular day. According to Aunt Zillah, Stanley Roy didn't cry when he was whipped but he jumped up sucking in air in pain and ran out of the classroom holding his shirt away from his back; Fagan had striped his skin with the strap.

I asked Aunt Zillah what that poor little boy who grew up to be my dad had done, but because he'd done something so trivial and because beatings were so common at the time, she couldn't even remember. However, Aunt Zillah did say:

> "I've *never forgotten that beating that poor Roy got. And dem boy – like Noel Archer* (Stanley Roy's younger brother) - *promised that any time dem catch that belt, they would mark it, mark it, mark it with a knife.*"

Their intention was to make several cuts on the belt to weaken it so that whenever Teacher Fagan used it to beat children again, pieces of it would fly off and it would do them less harm. Wishful thinking…

> "*But*" Aunt Zillah added, "*they could hardly catch Teacher Fagan's belt because he would always roll it up, put it in his pocket and take it home with him every day.*"

As is the way with Aunt Zillah, she carried on giving jokes but I couldn't really concentrate because I wanted to cry - and I still do just writing about it here. Imagine, enslaved people got stripes on their backs - but so did little 6-year old boys like Stanley Roy Archer decades later, despite their people surviving the brutality of slavery and having given up life itself for the freedom of such children.

[Archer Publishing 2009]

At the age of 77, the injustice of it all is still very fresh in Dad's mind. He's never told me about that particular incident – and I've never asked him to. But I'm sure there are also many other examples he could share.

So, is it little wonder that on more than one occasion, I heard my dad expressing a rather strong opinion on disciplining children? His comments were always something along these lines:

> "*Look, once a child is old enough to listen and understand, you just have to explain to them what they did wrong. There's no need to beat them once they reach a certain age. You just have to reason with them.*"

And he certainly remained true to that stance; just one look of absolute disappointment from my dad when I was a child was enough to make me cry bitterly and resolve never to do that thing again - and I was extremely well behaved.

Recently, dad and I shared some serious belly laughs over the telephone as he told me about Uncle Busha, Vin and Lucien's cousin – the amply named Woodham

Henry. The boy was <u>so</u> mischievous that they had to build a special desk for him on the teacher's platform so that the teacher could keep an eye on him at all times.

Now in those days, everyone used fountain pens which were filled with liquid ink. Stanley Roy boasts how he was one of the most skilled at carving pens from bamboo and he has always been admired for his carpentry skills. But the downside was that no-one liked to share their inkwell with Stanley Roy because his fountain pens always sucked up too much ink leaving very little for the others!

The teacher's ink was kept separately in a special cabinet behind his desk, but one day, somehow or other, Woodham Henry managed to get hold of the ink and - decided to urinate into the container. But when I asked why he'd do such a thing, dad could only reply:

> *"Him did just naughty; him just mek dat way - bad!"*

Woodham Henry had been his father's only child and we briefly discussed whether this fact may have had anything to do with his behaviour.

[Archer Publishing 2009]

Anyway, the boy carefully put the specially blended 'ink' back into the cabinet and as dad explained:

> *"It was there in the hot sun for days, festering and brewing. Eventually, Teacher Simmons needed to refill his fountain pen but he also wanted to find the source of the wrenkness* in the classroom.*
>
> *With all the children watching, he carefully examined the strange colour of the ink in the container. And my only thought was that perhaps teacher was wondering if it was ginger ale or something. But we all have a practice to shake something when we pick it up, don't we? But the ink was fermented and was ready to bubble over. So when Teacher opened it to put it up to his nose and smell it, he got a* <u>*proper*</u> *soaking!"*

Well – all hell broke loose that day! And all these years later, dad must've almost peed himself laughing as he told me the story – and I wasn't doing much better myself.

Now I'm still not absolutely sure of everything that actually happened following Teacher L.G. Simmons' soaking because dad was laughing so hard he couldn't speak clearly. But my own laughter dried up abruptly when dad told me how every single child in that huge classroom – "*innocent, one and all*" was severely punished as a result of that one school-boy prank. But why?

As dad tries to explain it, this incident happened prior to adult suffrage** when there was a very low rate of literacy in Jamaica so people were largely uneducated. But dad believes that sadly, even today, in spite of their relatively advanced literacy skills and education, teachers in Jamaica still lack an understanding of the concept of justice.

Dad informed me that apart from his own parents and the teachers -

> "*No outside people, even rich people, could beat us* (the Archer children) *due to our good behaviour because of the respect we had for our parents - and the respect everyone else had for our parents. Not even our uncles or aunties on either side would beat us.*

[Archer Publishing 2009]

My father would threaten us and say: 'As night come, I going to beat you!' But he never beat us. Whereas on the other hand, my mother <u>would</u> beat us - all three times a day! But we were very well behaved.

I remember one day, I was over the Bennett's place at their boiling house*** where they made wet or raw sugar. It's somewhere we would go and lots of boys who lived near by would come there. And I don't remember what happened, but I really thump up one of the boys and he ran home crying.

So the mother came marching back over to the boiling house with her son, like any pitcheery (phonetic) bird**** shouting: 'Which one ah dem? Which one of them?!' And all the boy ah tell her sey:***** 'Ah dat one deh!' – pointing me out – the woman kept going around and around hoping it wasn't me. So I said <u>'Me</u>!!'

I had a little cutlass in front of me – all of us Archers had a small cutlass which was given to us by our cousin to chop anything we wanted - like pineapple and so on. So she just turn down her head and go 'cross the hill, 'cross the stream and gone over into their area. She couldn't beat me!"

And the fearless Stanley Roy added:

"No matter how people big and bad, me NEVER 'fraid!

Master Plasterers of the 1960s!
(From left) **Uncle Isby, Uncle Vin Bennett and friend Jim plaster a ceiling in London**

In those times, there were no carrier bags and children never went to shop empty handed. Paper would be folded up in a certain way by shopkeepers to make a package for things like flour and sugar.

[Archer Publishing 2009]

And we would take a clean tablecloth to the shop to buy bread, so the shop keeper would wrap it up in that for your mother.

One day, my mother sent me to Poppy C's shop and he was trying to wrap up something for me but not doing a very good job. And before I knew it, the thought left my mind and travelled down to my mouth and the words: 'But Poppy C, yuh can't wrap!' fell right out!

Children didn't say such things to big people (adults) *so I knew I was wrong. He was the Sunday School teacher and as an older man, he was kind to children and had a good sense of humour - so he just laughed and admitted that he couldn't wrap at all.*

When I went home, I told my parents what had happened because I knew I did something wrong. But they didn't beat me. In fact, they laughed as well and agreed that Poppy C really couldn't wrap. But I knew that I had spoken out of turn."

Now a final word on Woodham Henry, who unlike Stanley Roy, really didn't seem to know when he'd just gone too far… maybe his big name made him believe he was a big man!

Dad and I did wonder whether his classmate had what is now called ADHD (Attention Deficit Hyperactivity Disorder). And dad continues to be amazed and saddened that even in 2009, Jamaica still had no educational provision in place for children with special needs. And they're only just beginning to discuss the needs of children with physical disabilities.

So, what happened to that little boy with the big name? Well, he did very well at school and was quiet bright. And dad recalls that Woodham Henry also came to England as a young man and went to live in Liverpool. He too was called up for National Service and went into the British Air Force, but he stayed on for an extra year. When he was demobbed, he went to live in London.

But then came Woodham Henry's downfall; following the breakdown of his marriage due to gambling, he ended up like a tramp****** on the streets. He wouldn't accept help from family or friends and not much long after, the sad news came that he'd been found dead on Clapham Common.

So, could children like Stanley Roy have actually learned anything from teachers like L.G. Simmons and S.W. Fagan? And what happened to such teachers as colonial education was modernised and began to improve?

NOTES

* Wrenkness – Jamaican patois for 'stench'

** Adult Suffrage came in 1944 and all Jamaicans over the age of 21 were granted the right to vote even if they were illiterate.

*** A basic type of sugar factory where sugar cane was boiled down to make sugar.

**** A type of bird with a black-coloured head, black eyes, white underbelly, large black beak and makes its nest as high up as possible in the tallest palm trees. It makes a very loud, distinctive screeching noise.

***** Ah tell her sey – Jamaican patois for 'was telling her that'.

****** A term that was commonly used for homeless people in earlier times.

CHAPTER FIVE

"Awakening to Politics"
A colonial education

Teacher L.G. Simmons was also the headmaster of Jeffrey Town Elementary School and his class was huge as it included classes 4, 5 and 6. As well as heading up the local school, Teacher was also running for office as a Labour MP in Jamaica. He went on to become the first ever person in Western St Mary (dad's district) to run for office and he was elected as an MP in Jamaica's very first elections following adult suffrage. But first, he was Stanley Roy's lowly teacher.

Every morning, 'The Gleaner' newspaper was thrown into the school yard and Teacher L.G. Simmons would read it out loud "*for his own use*" – as though he was really only reading it for the purposes of dictation for his pupils. And as dad rightly asked:

> *"Which child could possibly write down everything he was saying?"*

In fact, which adult could have done that even if they'd have been using a computer?!

[Archer Publishing 2009]

Anyway, Stanley Roy could understand the news and learned what was happening via Teacher and his *Gleaner*, but as a result of 'dictation', dad says he was always a poor speller. Even as a child, Stanley Roy was able to conclude that…

> "*Teacher didn't give a shit about who was following, who fell behind or who was beside him. He had his own axe to grind.*"

Eventually, L.G. Simmons progressed from being an MP and became the Minister of Education. No comment.

Once L.G. Simmons had left Jeffrey Town, his post was temporarily filled by Mr Burke. He was a retired teacher from Lucky Hill (about 3 miles from Jeffrey Town) *"who rode a grey horse"*. His wife Lily Mae Burke was a JP for the area (a Justice of the Peace) and she went on to become a well known activist within many women's movements across Jamaica.

Next, the young Mr S.W. Fagan filled the post, who we've already heard something of. He was from the parish of St Ann's and according to both dad and his school friend Aunt Zillah, Mr Fagan was a good teacher because he had attended a good college and even tried to teach them music. Perhaps this is why dad has always felt that the arts are a vital part of a child's education, along with travelling and he always encouraged me to learn and play music throughout life. And dad still takes great pleasure in knowing that I'm musical, classically trained and even worked as a professional musician and singer.

Dad even became a devoted committee member of the Salterton Music Centre where I attended orchestra and all sorts of instrumental lessons in the evenings after school. I even went to the club on Saturday mornings as I got older when I'd sing pop and show songs with the teenage club members.

SIX—ISLINGTON GAZETTE FRIDAY SEPTEMBER 27 1974

16 years of music

MISS Amelia Percival, founder of the Holloway-based Salterton Music Centre, cuts the 16th birthday cake while the young musicians, parents and teachers look on. Cutting the cake with her is four-year-old Gerald Adigun, son of Mr Gerald Adigun, sitting next to him, who donated the cake. The country's first ever music centre brings lessons and playing to young people who could not otherwise afford it.

[Archer Publishing 2009]

In the above newspaper clipping from the Islington Gazette, Yvonne – the budding violinist – appears sitting 2nd from the left in the 2nd row. The picture was taken in Grafton School's upstairs hall back in 1974 and Stanley Roy has cherished this weathered and fading treasure ever since...

Teacher S.W. Fagan eventually left Jeffrey Town to become the headmaster of a school in Old Harbour. And some years later when Stanley Roy went there to build a classroom (remember, he has talents in many trades) he saw Teacher Fagan's servant who was still working with him.

"The servant went and told Teacher that I was there and he introduced me to the children as one of his old pupils who was very good at maths."

Up until today, dad maintains that maths and languages are the most important subjects in education and that maths is a particularly wonderful subject because there can only be one correct answer. So Stanley Roy enjoyed a very proud moment that day in Old Harbour - but perhaps it's worth remembering that this was the same

Teacher Fagan who had given him a brutal whipping some years before.

Dad also remembers the long benches that pupils sat at in the school room and how pupils from different classes would sit next to each other so that pupils couldn't cheat or copy from one another. Miss Reynolds was a "*red woman*"* or mulatto from the parish** of either Manchester or St Elizabeth, and she became Stanley Roy's teacher when he about 9 years old.

During maths, Miss Reynolds would often say:

> *"Huh! Mr Archer has finished his sums. I'm sure they're right; he's a great man!"*

I like to think that she really understood Sir Roy's potential. And because Miss Reynolds didn't want this great little man to be bored once he'd finished his work and wanted to reward him…

> *"She would send me to sit out under the plum tree where it was cool. I used to finish my work so quickly that I knew I was bright."*

And what would Sir Roy do under the plum tree to entertain himself?

[Archer Publishing 2009]

> *"I would just watch people and pickney (children) go past."*

It really didn't take much to entertain children in those days! And Stanley Roy is also proud to report:

> *"On my first day in A Class, Teacher borrowed me to answer a question about the scripture*** to put the 1st class students to shame. I did so well that I skipped my class and went straight up to B Class! I'll never forget that!"*

Of course, Jamaica belonged to Britain and the schooling system was British. So, is it little wonder that Stanley Roy couldn't understand why the same rules didn't apply to schools in England, when he got there, including mine****?

> *"When you were small, the teacher called me to the school and told me I shouldn't teach you anything! I shouldn't teach you at home because she can't teach you anything in the class.*
>
> *Maybe the sensible thing to do would have been to give you different work to do. That really hurt me, telling me not to teach my own child anything. It was stupid. But at the time, I was on my own with you and*

I couldn't afford to send you to a private school. There were about 3 schools in London for what we would call 'genius' children but as your mother wasn't around, I couldn't afford to send you. I was alone."

It is my wish that my dad would stop feeling so saddened by this; after all, that was years ago and we did the best we could with what we had – and we really didn't do so badly, did we?

By the end of Primary School, the headmaster, Mr Marshall, had ambitious ideas for Mr Archer's daughter:

"Mr Marshall said: 'Mr Archer, the two best schools in North London are Highbury Hill High and Camden High' – which was beside the Jewish Free School. And he said he was going to send a letter with your papers to Mrs Butcher - the headmistress at Highbury - who he knew. He was sure you could get in with your good behaviour, training and with being bright. I was never called to school for bad behaviour, lateness or anything."

As we've discovered, dad's own education up until the age of 14 had proved more than adequate for him to become a valuable worker, soldier and citizen for Britain. He read the newspapers religiously, especially what he called 'the scandal sheet' on a Sunday (*The News of the World*), because he said it gave the facts of each story whether the people involved were rich or poor.

I suspect that reading the newspaper and an interest in the news, current affairs and politics stemmed from his early experiences of Teacher L.G. Simmons reading articles to his class from *The Jamaican Gleaner*. So, that was reading. Dad impressively used a pocket dictionary for writing letters and it obviously impressed other people too. He reminded me how, as a small child, I'd often ask why so many people were always ringing our doorbell and wanting him to explain, read or fill in something or the other for them. I simply couldn't understand why.

"Why does everyone have to come to you, dad?" I would ask. Perhaps I was jealous.

If dad's hands were wet or he was cooking or gardening, as was the norm, I would be drafted in. The adults would sometimes tell me that they didn't have their glasses with them so, could I read something or the other for them? I often felt flattered at the praise and their marvelling at my excellent reading and would be happily 'fooled' into doing it again and again. A neighbour even asked me to help his daughter of a similar age with her school work because she wasn't doing well!

As an adult, it's now clear that many of dad's friends had also left school at 14 and perhaps even younger in some cases. But of course, not everyone had quite mastered reading and writing sufficiently enough to feel confident about facing the world of officialdom without some assistance.

Even dad's Greek millionaire friends recognised his intellectual abilities and wisdom and they would consult him on plans to improve their properties etc. But what dad probably remembers most about them are the rewards for the help he provided – holidays with them to Cyprus, jobs, and certainly a lot of respect, which was obvious whenever I met them. And much of this was thanks to his education. So, where might life have taken Stanley Roy Archer if he'd had the opportunity to continue studying beyond the age of 14?

Anyway, dad would often go to his Greek friends' homes where there'd be 2 chickens on the spit, roasting with corn on the cob. And wine and whisky were the accompaniments.

"And when we finished our business as men, one of the wifes might call out: 'Yoo hoo – dinner is ready!' And when I would tell them no thanks, I really couldn't eat anything more, Jack or whoever would look inna me face like to say - you insult my wife; you have to eat!"

Following one particular feast, dad couldn't eat properly for 6 days. I have memories of him drinking Andrews liver salts and belching and groaning with discomfort! But I believe that such experiences and his wide range of friends and colleagues from different backgrounds and cultures really helped dad to further his education. And let's not forget what he'd learned through National Service!

NOTES

* Someone of a lighter skin tone than the majority of Jamaicans. 'Mulattoes' is an old term used to describe people of 'mixed race'.

** Jamaica is divided up into 14 parishes or areas.

*** Scripture – passage(s) from the Christian Bible.

**** Yvonne attended Grafton School from nursery up until Primary School level; it's now a Beacon School.

CHAPTER SIX
"Defender of the Weak"
Bashing the Black on the square

Unlike Gunner Archer, the only other Black man in his battalion <u>was</u> educated - and also unlike Gunner Archer, he was "*soft*". So guess who had to defend him? The guy from St Vincent was teased "*mercilessly*" throughout square bashing and as Gunner Archer put it:

> "*One Lance Corporal rough him up <u>bad</u> man, and say all kinds of things to him.*"

As history shows, whether it was wartime or peace time, fearless Jamaicans often came to the rescue. It was groups of Jamaican men who went to the defence of others across London in places like Notting Hill when the Teddy Boys of the 1950s thought they were bad enough to beat up and even kill black men in the street for no reason.

Remember, it was the Notting Hill race riots of 1958 and the murder of Kelso Cochrane, a man from Antigua [ref 3 page 184] on May 17th 1959* by a gang of white men, which inspired Claudia Jones [ref 4 page 184] to establish the

Notting Hill Carnival in August of the same year. She did this in the spirit of building peace and community cohesion. Fifty years on, the Notting Hill Carnival is still taking place and is celebrated as Europe's biggest street carnival. And here, it's worth noting that these memoirs have been created as part of a peace project with similar objectives.

So how did someone like Stanley Roy Archer get to be so fearless? Well, we've already heard how he was a rather resilient little boy, but perhaps this story will also help to answer that question:

"As a teenager, against my father's advice, I went to Cascade** to work for a Pastor on his property. He wanted a cow pasture to be cleaned for Christmas but when I got there, he also wanted me to clean up around a valuable lime tree. That was a big piece of hard work but he leaned up on his long gun and said: "Bad foot" - so we wouldn't be getting any help from him.

So I told the others and then him – 'look man, that's a different job!' And he answered, "Shut up or I will shut you up" – meaning, with his gun. And he told me not to come up in the yard.

I went up close to him with my red, sharp cutlass – so he couldn't shoot me with his long gun because I was too close for him to use it. But he started saying…'Likkle short boy, nuh***…' But I was so close that if a mosquito bite him and he shift his position, he was a goner.

My father <u>did</u> tell me not to go, but I still went to the job. And the man could've shot me and nothing would happen because he had money and I was poor. He was one of those brown, feisty**** people."

It was the same young man who'd been ready to take on a rich Pastor with a big gun, despite being armed with nothing other than a sharp, red farmer's cutlass, who became Gunner Archer. Here was a man who was eager to work yet wasn't afraid to lose his job in standing up for everyone's rights.

And it was he, The Fearless One, who had a word with the Lance Corporal about bullying the other Black soldier

[Archer Publishing 2009]

during square bashing. But it wasn't a quiet word; no, it was a very loud, deliberate word - in front of everyone! The Lance Corporal was told in no uncertain terms…

"If you continue to taunt him, I will "tek your f*&^^ head mek football!!"

The Lance Corporal understood immediately, but he didn't dare report Gunner Archer because of his build and strength – and abuse of the guy from St Vincent stopped immediately.

Oddly enough, following that little 'meeting', Gunner Archer earned even more respect from his entire battalion. We've wondered what happened to that man from St Vincent, but so far, we've been unable to trace him.

NOTES

* These memoirs mark 50 years since the murder of Kelso Cochrane, 50 years since the start of the Notting Hill Carnival and 50 years since the official end of the conflict in Cyprus.

** Cascade is near Ocho Rios in Jamaica - a seaside tourist area.

*** 'nuh' – Jamaican patois for 'don't'.

**** 'feisty' – Jamaican patois for cheeky, disrespectful, arrogant.

Stanley Roy with 'all the boys' at his passing out ceremony at Kiwi Gordon Barracks, Bulford, Wiltshire in 1957. Does anyone know who the other Black gunner might be?

CHAPTER SEVEN
"Keeper of the Peace"
Why Cyprus?

When twelve weeks of square bashing finally came to an end, Gunner Archer of the 25th Field Regiment Royal Artillery was sent out on active duty to Cyprus from Bulford in Wilshire. The year was 1957.

> *"The boys were shit-scared of going on active duty because an advanced party had gone out to set up camp before we left England, but they were blown up. But I just told them: look, if there's one man coming back to Blighty alive, it's me!"*

There was a raging civil war in full swing between the Greek and the Turkish Cypriots. According to the records of a House of Commons sitting on the 31st of January 1956 [ref 1 page 176] there was already 7,800 men doing their National Service out there. And by the official end of the 'emergency' on 31st March 1959 - 35,000 British troops in total had served in Cyprus.

At another sitting on the 3rd of July 1956, [ref 1 page 176] questions were being asked of Mr Anthony Head, the then Secretary of State for War, whether 12 weeks of basic training were enough to prepare young lads for their experiences in Cyprus. Considering the fact that policemen received at least 19 weeks of training before being sent out onto the relatively calm streets of London, this probably seemed a fair enough question to many. But Commons questions aside, young men like Stanley Roy were still sent out to swell the ranks during a dangerous civil war – the Northern Ireland of the day.

Leisure time on the ship crossing the Mediterranean to Cyprus; the men were only allowed to wear plimsolls on deck to protect it. (1957)

Growing up, I always wondered why the Greek and Turkish Cypriots didn't get along, but I never seemed to get an answer from my father – despite him holding the most information on this of all the adults I knew.

I only learned that the Cypriot issue was something that was hush-hush, taboo – so I asked few blatant questions,  somehow understanding that the wounds were still very fresh.

I had both Greek and Turkish Cypriot school mates at Grafton and we all played together in the playground. From my limited understanding, their parents all came from the same island, just like Jamaicans all came from the same island - only Jamaicans weren't fighting each other.

Eventually, I managed to distinguish a few truths for myself although they weren't strictly relevant to the conflict; my Greek friends seemed to follow the Greek Christian Orthodox faith and like the priest on our road, lots of adults dressed in black a lot of the time. But my Turkish school mates were Muslims and in their chip shop on Tollington Way, they certainly didn't sell 'savaloy' sausages. So, that satisfied my childish intellect for a time, although I still couldn't work out why any of those differences meant that their parents should be sworn, bitter enemies.

With the arrival of 2009, 50 years after the official end to the 'Cyprus Emergency', we felt it was time to add just a little flesh and a different perspective to the bones of this story and attempt to tackle a prickly topic. By doing this, we hope that Stanley Roy's vivid account of his National Service on Murder Mile will help to add some clarity and bring to life this period in our shared history.

It is also our desire and reasonable demand that the contributions of Black people like Stanley Roy Archer be recognized and embedded within British historical archives. Anyways…

[Archer Publishing 2009]

In a nutshell, what we now know is that Cyprus was inhabited by both Greek and Turkish Cypriots and the Greek Cypriots were fighting for independence from Britain as well as for unity with Greece [ref 5 page 185]. The Turkish Cypriots were totally against such an idea. It can't be overstated at this point how high and deep feelings ran on this issue and a state of emergency was declared by Britain in November 1955 as a result.

The situation lead to the Greek Cypriots establishing EOKA [ref 6 page 185] (*Ethniki Organosis Kyprion Agoniston* meaning National Organization of Cypriot Fighters) under George Grivos [ref 7 page 185] and supported by Archbishop Makarios [ref 8 page 185]. The organisation launched bloody attacks against both the Turks and the British troops in a fight for independence from Britain and in the opinion of Stanley Roy – "*they were very smart*". But along with the Brits and the Turks, he still thinks of EOKA as "*terrorists*". The group members described themselves as 'freedom fighters' and are reportedly reflected as such in Greek history.

Following intense and prolonged attacks by the EOKA, the Turks felt forced into forming their own underground organisation, the TMT (*Türk Mukavemet Teskilati* meaning The Turkish Resistance Organization). And reportedly, the organisation also wanted to ensure that Britain was aware that the Turks also held some power. Although we've not found much information on the TMT, we can rest assured that its formation was an additional complication to the conflict in Cyprus and made it even more heated.

A bombed vehicle back at base camp (Photo by Gunner Archer)

The island of Cyprus would go on to gain independence from Britain in 1960. But who would be in charge – the Greek or the Turkish Cypriots? Eventually, an agreement was reached and they were forced to share the island, with the exception of 99 miles which would remain the property of Britain until Parliament decided otherwise.

[Archer Publishing 2009]

But before this agreement was made, people like Gunner Archer were sent out to Cyprus as part of the British peace-keeping effort - although he is convinced that they weren't always as neutral as they claimed to be. And he believes that some spying was probably taking place.

Anyway, despite the dangers, the troops were not totally confined to their army barracks, so the British armed forces did get opportunities to explore Cyprus in their own way.

"We never mixed much with the locals because it could've led to a lot of problems and we could have been blown up or shot. But I wasn't involved in too much of the hand fighting; I helped on both sides", dad explained, which brought it home to me that his life was in very real danger out there every single day. By 1959, 274 British soldiers had lost their lives.

"But they (the army) used to arrange trips for us. Sometimes they would put on a truck to take us into mainly Turkish villages where it would be fairly safe for an evening out. We would spend the evening there drinking brandy, which was very cheap, and

KEO beer. And some of soldiers used to get so drunk that we'd have to put them up to the front of the cab on the floor and cover them with our feet so nobody could see them and charge them for being drunk when we got back to the camp."

The army also organised trips for the troops to Famagusta, but they had to stay within the city walls. As dad describes it:

"The walls were 10 feet wide and made of stone with archways in it. I could just see it and imagine they would've had horse and carts or even camels going through the archways while soldiers would march on top of the walls on guard duty.

There were some big guns mounted on the walls facing out to sea but they were ancient, so they weren't in service – but, they gave me a good picture of what a city wall must've looked like in Biblical days.

They had different social activities during the trips to Famagusta and the food was mostly barbecued lamb, goat and sometimes pork in the Greek villages.. They also had pitta bread – kebab bread as we now call it - and plenty of vegetables - and oranges, melons, pomegranate or pongonut (phon as called in Jamaica). And I'll never forget the strong smell of Turkish coffee and the smoke from the barbecues.

I never went on any trips with the big truck as I never got back in time to leave with the others from ambulance duties with the doctor so they detailed a smaller vehicle to take a few of us who couldn't leave early enough, such as the cook and maybe a few others plus a guard.

The Greek villages were prosperous and progressive and they had the best part of the island. But we also went into the Turkish city part. But after they dropped us off there, we would take a taxi out to the Greek part to get a different type of entertainment. There, they weren't as stern religiously, and they had more entertainment out in Murder Mile.

Some of Gunner Archer's fellow soldiers at base camp (Picture taken by Gunner Archer)

In the villages, they were all Muslims so we couldn't even look at the young girls. And I'll tell you a story about that: a group of young veiled girls were coming towards some soldiers and when the girls saw them, they went over a wall and hid.

Of course, some of the soldiers didn't understand the culture and were mischievous so they jumped on the wall and looked over there at them. And this caused a <u>big</u> stir which could have been very dangerous for us - and the soldiers were confined to barracks as a *punishment for quite a long time. I wasn't there but I understood about the culture."*

And how were British soldiers received in Cyprus? As it was the Northern Ireland of the day, I really wondered…

"The Turkish people welcomed the British army every time, any where, all the time. The Greek people were a bit different because in my opinion, we were more one-sided because I felt that the army was fighting more on the Turkish side.

I was driving an Army Champ with a body made by Austin and an engine made by Rolls Royce but it looked like a Land Rover, just not as high; it was more compact. But because of my position, I was driving the doctor because of the Geneva Convention, any place where we were called to help in a medical emergency in any type of village – and we were driving in an ambulance with the Red Cross international symbol on it – we were well received with plenty of food and protection. They would escort us in and out.

There were quite a lot of baby cases – deliveries or to look after sick babies – and the people were glad to see us then and they would chat to us about everything - like they want to know where you come from and they would feed us."

At this point, I wondered whether dad was ever treated strangely or differently by the Cypriots being a Black man on the island. Were people staring at him like they stare at Black people in parts of Europe and the UK today?

"No. Black people had always been in Cyprus - Greece and Turkey, so they weren't surprised to see me there, only maybe a few of the younger ones.

There was one other Black man in our battalion who was posted to my regiment but not in my battery so he was in a different area of Cyprus. I would see that Black man when I drove the doctor to the other Battery Units to give people medical attention. He was also a driver and a Gunner but he wasn't a Jamaican, he was from another British-owned Caribbean island.

In the bars or coffee shops in the Turkish villages, they sold Turkish coffee although I think it was really Greek coffee. But they also sold beer and brandy. Sometimes they played music – a banjo type music - and they sang in Turkish. But in Famagusta, there was more of a variety of entertainment. Without going into details, you could get 'everything and anything' down there. I think we'll just leave it at that."

Gunner Archer sits atop his Army Champ at base camp in Cyprus. It's clearly marked with the internationally recognised Red Cross symbol on the front.

CHAPTER EIGHT

"The Survivor"

National Service on Murder Mile

As we've heard, Gunner Archer was the doctor's driver –
and the doctor was a posh officer!

> "*There was a rule that if we're being fired on, we
> should let the people disembark, put the vehicle in
> a safe place and return fire."*

But before they left the relative safety of base camp, the
doctor would often ask:

> "*Now what do we do if we come under fire, Archer?
> Do we stand and return fire?"*

And Gunner Archer would dutifully answer:

> "*No sir! We drive like the f&*^% wind!"*

And the doc's reaction was always favourable –

> "*Excellent! Good Man! Off we go!"* - and other

expressions of true British grit and approval to that effect.

And that proved to be some of the best advice Gunner
Archer would ever receive in Famagusta. In fact, it
probably saved his life on more than one occasion -
especially on those three infamous miles of road which
the troops had nick-named 'Murder Mile'.

And Gunner Archer passed the very same advice onto the new rookie doctor – a Welsh man called Brian. He was sent out to Cyprus straight after finishing medical school to replace the original medical officer who'd done his time on National Service. So Brian was very resentful about studying for so many years and not ever having had a chance to earn a penny before being sent out on active National Service duty.

Anyway, Gunner Archer and the new doc got to know each other pretty well because not long after he'd arrived in Cyprus, the change of climate gave the doc a really bad cold so it fell to Gunner Archer to look after him.

Gunner Archer soon settled into army life and it was good to him in some ways. Personally, he never encountered any discrimination in his all-white environment and the Scottish and English soldiers who shared his tent made two great roomies. And because of 'Dan Archer', they always had the best tent – the place where all the other soldiers went to have fun!

Gunner Archer sometimes earned extra money by being the battalion's barber – short back and sides being an army requirement. But this was an informal arrangement:

"Although I never charged the men, I would leave a beret out and they would drop money in."

Gunner Archer had taken up his new role after the Turkish man who used to cut hair, simply disappeared one day…

"We had a good relationship, me and the Turkish barber, because he would hitch a ride with myself and the doc in the ambulance to the different battalions to cut everyone's hair. But the English

used to call him racist names and treat him very badly".

'Barber Archer' in action!

Later on, when he was back in London having done his time, Stanley Roy the civilian, heard his name being shouted out on the streets of Hornsey, North London. It was his old friend, the Turkish barber.

> "*Man, he was so glad to see me! He ran up to me and hug me up and laugh and then he carry me into a shop, where I think he must've found some work as a barber. And he introduced me to his brother and he other men in shop. He was really glad to see me!*"

[Archer Publishing 2009]

The English also hurled racist abuse at members of the Indian Abdu family who served them glasses of tea, *"banjos"'* (phonetic) which was what they called fried egg sandwiches, and chips.

> *"Apparently, because they had provided such excellent service to the British armed forces out in India, the Queen had honoured them by awarding them the contract to run the NAFAs. So that was good business for them."*

Later on, adding to his educational and military achievements, Gunner Archer passed a special driving course which meant that he got a pay rise. And for every £1 he earned, the army trebled it and put it on top to make it £4 – a lot of money in those days!

Serial No. **3**   Army Form A.2038

WAR DEPARTMENT DRIVING PERMIT

(Not valid for driving any mechanically propelled vehicle for private purposes)

Issued in accordance with current Army Council

Instructions.

The undersigned *GNR ARCHER. S.R.*

(description) *R.H.Q. BTY.*

25TH FLD. REGT. R.A.

being employed on Military Service is hereby authorised by the Army Council to drive mechanically propelled vehicles of :—

Group— A   B   C   ~~D~~   ~~E~~   ~~F~~   ~~G~~   ~~K~~

(Delete Groups inapplicable)

when on Government duty, from *26 OCT.*

19*58* until *25 JULY* 19*59*

G. W. Turner.

Permanent Under-Secretary of State for War.

R Archer .... Signature of Holder

Permit not valid without Unit Stamp and signature of Issuing Officer on reverse.

The army sent a lot of that money directly to his mother Elmore (Aunt More) and his father Jeremiah Archer who were exceptional and unconventionally modern parents for their time. They were his official dependents and Aunt More used the money to pay school expenses for Stanley Roy's young son Ernel* plus all Stanley Roy's younger brothers, sisters and several nieces and nephews – all of whom lived at 'top yard' - our Grandmother's home. And of course, the money was also used to support everyone in lots of other ways.

JF

NATIONAL SERVICE GRANTS
MINISTRY OF PENSIONS AND NATIONAL INSURANCE
NORCROSS, BLACKPOOL, LANCS.

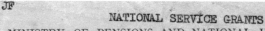

Telephone : Thornton 2371
Telegraphic Address : Warpension, Blackpool.

Our Ref. A93705 H   *Your Ref.*

12th August, 1957.

Dear Sir,

I am writing with regard to the application for a National Service grant made by you on your mother's behalf.

In order that we may proceed with the claim, it would be appreciated if you would kindly state the weekly or monthly amount of any contribution made by you to your mother prior to your call-up, and also forward any documentary evidence in support of this.

An addressed label is attached for your use.

Yours faithfully,

[signature] Hillis

for Controller.

23409344 Gunner Archer, Stanley,
R.A.

> **An official letter asking for proof of Gunner Archer's dependants in order to process his claim**

Sadly, Jeremiah passed away and was buried while his son was back in England but hadn't yet been demobbed – officially dismissed from the army. This was a great source of sadness and resentment for Stanley Roy, especially as he didn't even have a photograph of his father.

Previously, he'd gone to great lengths to buy and send a Kodak box camera along with film and the instructions all the way from Cyprus to Jamaica to ensure that he had a decent photograph of his parents. This was the only request he'd ever asked of his family and they hadn't granted it - something he never forgot. A photograph of my grandfather does not exist.

But Aunt More was certainly alive and kicking and she had a family of Archers to raise – with or without her beloved Uncle Jerry. Born in 1900, Aunt More was the kind of woman who really knew how to stretch an English pound!** The children at top yard were always known, amongst other things, for how beautifully turned out they were in their original, matching 'Elmore' designer gear.

Len and cousins outside the Archer family home 'Top Yard' – the 1ˢᵗ in the district built from concrete blocks

And many years later, supported by foreign currency from her sons in Britain and Canada, Aunt More's house became the most beautiful and modern in the district. She even enjoyed the delights of a cuckoo clock, courtesy of Stanley Roy, and her television set was the first ever in the district! This became a firm favourite with the family dog, a deaf St Bernard, and always lead to countless number of eyes peering through the windows each evening!

NOTES

* Ernel was also known as 'Len' and later, 'Ringo'.

** *As a British owned island, Jamaica used the same currency as Britain.*

CHAPTER NINE
"*The Classy Man*"
A privileged soldier

As well as providing anyone in their designated area with medical assistance, Gunner Archer and the doctor also spent their time rescuing wounded British troops. But they also had the gruesome task of picking up dead bodies - and body parts. Yet surprisingly, when they arrived back at base camp in the evenings, they were still hungry!

The common mess hall was always closed by the time they arrived, so the doctor ordered that Gunner Archer's supper should always be served in the officer's dining hall. He was the only lowly soldier allowed to eat there and the menu, wine and champagne list never ceased to amaze him. Could they really be at war?

It was in the officer's dining hall out there in Cyprus where Gunner Archer was taught how to appreciate and drink champagne. He insisted that "*regular champagne did taste bad*" – no matter how expensive it was - and he wasted many a glass. So in exasperation, the doctor introduced him to pink champagne and from then on, that was it! Throughout the years, it's been pink champagne for Mr Archer – or no champagne at all!

The other thing about the army which must have made other troops jealous of Gunner Archer was that once he'd arrived back to England and was waiting to be demobbed, he was never assigned any weekend duties. And perhaps this was a blessing in disguise because it was then that he received the very sad news of his father's sudden death rather than amidst the surreal way of life out on Murder Mile.

The 25th Field Regiment Artillery was based out in Wiltshire for a few months during the summer of 1959 once they'd returned from Cyprus, so it was there that they were ordered to wait for their official release from National Service. There was one sergeant who lived out in Hounslow, but for some reason, he would only drive from that Hounslow Station to his home. And guess who he requested as his chauffeur to transport him back and forth between base camp to Hounslow at the start and end of each weekend?

So Gunner Archer proved lucky once again!

He was at home in London every weekend having fun, and unlike the rest of his regiment, he didn't have to undertake any military duties. Of course, Gunner Archer had no complaints!

But let's get back to that lovely civil war in Cyprus…

[Archer Publishing 2009]

CHAPTER TEN
"The Brave Man"
A memorable call out

One evening, just as Gunner Archer and his medical officer were about to tuck into a delicious three course meal, they were called out. Some top, high ranking Colonel or his driver had come under heavy fire on Murder Mile and they'd been wounded. So off went Gunner Archer and the doc to rescue them.

As usual, Gunner Archer drove so fast along that stretch that…

> "D*em have fart fi catch mi!"*

Hell, even the bullets had 'fart fi catch im'!

> "*And the sound that my vehicle made when I was drawing gear and pressing gas* was such, that dem tink ah low-flying aircraft!"*

When they arrived at the spot, the Colonel's driver was so badly wounded that Gunner Archer had to set off a smoke flare to signal for a helicopter. The driver was flown to Nicosia Hospital, but the next day when Gunner Archer and the doctor asked for enquiries to be made about him, they were told that unfortunately, the young man had died en route. The flat, canvas stretcher they'd used to carry him on had been so bloodied that it had to be burned. So that was Murder Mile.

As for the Colonel, he was already deceased by the time Gunner Archer and the Medical Officer reached him. So they loaded him onto a stretcher and Gunner Archer secured the stretcher in the back of the jeep with three or four gun slings. And all this while, bullets flew around them.

The vehicle the colonel and his driver were bombed in
(Picture taken by Gunner Archer)

[Archer Publishing 2009]

Just as they were about ready to tear up those tyres and get back to base, a high-ranking officer came up to Gunner Archer:

"*Are you the driver?*" he asked.

"*Yes* Sir!" Gunner Archer replied.

And handing him something wrapped up in a blanket, the officer added:

"*Here is the Colonel's foot.*"

They'd found the foot using a sniffer dog. Gunner Archer unceremoniously threw it into the back of his Army Champ** and kissing his teeth and uttering more than a few Jamaican expletives across the gunfire, he jumped in behind the wheel.

Off they went down the notorious stretch of Murder Mile Road, swerving and bumping along. But the Colonel kept rolling off his stretcher and into the back of the vehicle.

"*The Colonel was a large man and him shake like jelly. So I couldn't leave him like that in the back just in case he shook and rolled right out onto the road. And then who was going to have to get out to pick him up?!*"

So risking life and limb for a man who was already dead, Gunner Archer screeched to a stop and using his own gun slings- plus two extra that he borrowed - he did what had to be done:

> "*I girth the Colonel like donkey and tell him 'Move now, if yuh tink you blood**f^& bad!* "

And perhaps the Colonel heard the threat because he stayed put and Gunner Archer somehow got himself and the Doc back to base in one piece – and lived to tell the tale.

NOTES

* 'Drawing gear and pressing gas' - changing gears and accelerating.
** An Army Champ was the make of vehicle used as an ambulance at the time, and it was clearly marked with the international Red Cross symbol.

CHAPTER ELEVEN
"A Dead Funny Man"
A night with the Colonel

As usual, despite all the blood, gore, guts and even a gruesome foot on this occasion – Gunner Archer and the doc were still hungry. And after a hearty meal, Gunner Archer was ready for his bunk. But before he could get there, he found out that he'd been awarded the 'honour' of staying up all night to guard the Colonel. Now the Colonel may have felt honoured by such an arrangement, but do you really think Gunner Archer felt the same?!

He's never been able to explain why he had to guard the poor Colonel when it was blatantly obvious that he wasn't ever going to leave base camp or go anywhere again this life. Hell, the man was even missing a foot so he wouldn't have even been able to walk anyway! But, those were Gunner Archer's orders, so like a good British soldier he resentfully stayed in the MT park all night – the Millitary Transport vehicles' parking area. And the Colonel comfortably 'slept' the night away in a nearby 3-ton lorry!

Many of us might well have been spooked out by such night duty, and not have been able to sleep a wink. But Gunner Archer says…

> *"Yes, I did manage to get some sleep. Him gone – and once a man dead…"*

Yes, the Colonel was definitely deceased, but one side-effect of that infamous night watch was that unfortunately, for once, poor Gunner Archer was off his food for a few days. And he couldn't even enjoy a decent glass of pink champagne. Perhaps that was payback for girthing the Colonel like a donkey!

[Archer Publishing 2009]

CHAPTER TWELVE

"The Husband and Father"

Back to reality and life on Civvy Street

PART I

Come 1959, Gunner Archer had completed his 2 years of National Service. But pleased with his performance, or perhaps simply still in need of troops to swell the ranks in the region, the 25th Field Regiment Artillery requested that Gunner Archer stay on for an extra year and take a promotion following his success with that special driving course. He'd become invaluable and was one of the Royal Sergeant Major's favourites.

RSM* Bailey had been promoted to Warrant Officer for having served in many countries. As dad explained:

> *"He got a pip on his shoulder in Cyprus and his chest was <u>covered</u> with medals. He had a crown on his leather band on his wrist and he was responsible for discipline."*

The men were afraid of RSM Bailey so no-one could quite understand what he and the doc's driver, a young Black man from Jamaica, had in common. Everyone wondered why they enjoyed talking about the RSM's travels around the world so much – from Africa where he was fighting the Mau-Maus in Kenya** (ref 9 page 185) to Asia.

Once, a man who dad believes had been a governor or had held some other high position in Jamaica and had then taken command of all the land forces in Cyprus, visited base camp. He hadn't been an army person, but after greeting RSM Bailey, he went over to speak with Gunner Archer.

No-one could understand why they had such a long chat!

> *"He was a gentleman and he asked me which part of the world I was from, where I lived in London and if I liked it in the army."*

And what was Gunner Archer's response?

> *"Well, I told him that I was, you know, making the best of it. I wasn't going to say anything else!"*

And what else could the gentleman have expected Gunner Archer to say? 'Yes, the army is the real reason why I moved to Britain'?

Or 'Yes, it's great fun running up and down Murder Mile and staring death in the face every day'?

RSM Bailey is 2nd from the left, marked 'X' and the 'gentleman' with the Jamaican connection is speaking with him.

During one of their conversations, RSM Bailey advised Gunner Archer that if he stayed on in the army for an extra year, he might get a 'cushty' posting. And he explained how British Honduras, which became Belize following independence, and Hong Kong, were the best postings because they were free, quiet, peaceful – and a lot of fun. But who knows where Gunner Archer might have been sent.

Anyway, Gunner Archer wasn't thinking about having fun abroad by now, so his response was basically 'Thanks, but no thanks'. He'd seen enough death and on a practical level, he explained:

"*I wanted to get back to Blighty - back to Civvy Street*" - a civilian dressed in all his fashionable clothes, dancing jazz and ballroom with his Jamaican friends to music provided by big bands across London's West End. And he never forgot the <u>real</u> reason why he'd left Jamaica for England in the first place:

"*I wanted to work and send money home.*"

Stanley Roy Archer certainly hadn't left Jamaica in 1954 to go on active duty for National Service. And he hadn't left so that he could join the British Army. The conflict, in which he was ordered to drive along Murder Mile and back several times a day, had nothing to do with him as far as he was concerned. And delightful as it was, Stanley Roy Archer hadn't travelled to England to learn how to appreciate pink champagne in Europe either.

"*I just wanted to get on with life*" he said.

And boy, did he do that!!

NOTES

* RSM – Royal Sergeant Major

** The Mau Maus of Kenya fought against British Rule; Britain declared a
state of emergency and sent out reinforcement troops in 1952

PART II

By the winter of 1959, Stanley Roy was back in
London and living at the same address he'd lived at
before he left for Cyprus - 163 Caledonian Road. He
transferred from the Underground to the buses and
was based at the Highgate Trolley Bus Garage. It was
there that he met my mother Hortense, who was his
pretty conductress, and by 1960, they were married.

One of their trolley bus
routes was along the
Kingsway and just as they
do today, buses terminated
outside the BBC's Bush
House on the Strand.
Stanley Roy still remembers
how people inside the BBC
hated seeing Black people
even walk across the front steps of Bush House - so it's
been a marvel and an absolute pleasure for him to know

122

that his own daughter ended up working <u>inside</u> that building for many years – and not as a cleaner!

During the summer of 2005, dad and I went along to a talk which featured Brenda Emmanus, a BBC London Arts Correspondent, at BBC Television Centre. And dad took great delight in explaining how he had been so surprised to see a Black woman in charge at reception in Bush House - and why!

While he was waiting for me, the woman had sent a colleague - a white man - to fetch him some cold water on a particularly hot day! For dad, this was a truly astonishing thing to witness, so he continues to tell the story to all who'll listen to help them understand how Britain has changed.

Anyway, back to the 1960s…

The newly weds, Mr and Mrs Archer, lived at 50 Eburne Road (*see picture above*) and then moved onto 15 Windsor Road which was owned by 'Big Granny' (Uncle Isby and Uncle Lowell's mum). Finally, they moved to 55 Windsor Road, almost opposite Granny. Dad obviously liked the area; Holloway was fairly quiet, it had good shops and great transport links – plus, he knew all his neighbours.

The year was 1963 and they'd managed to buy their very first home for a staggering £4,500! His first priority was to put in a bathroom – something rarely found in houses at the time. So people like dad were accustomed to going to the Hornsey Road Public Baths for showers while others bathed in tin tubs in their kitchens. But Stanley Roy had had enough; Jamaicans were used to showering or bathing every day back home in their own country.

And to give me more of a flavour of what life was like during those days, Stanley Roy went on to explain:

"Youth was in my favour. I lived very well – good food, drink and parties and we went to good places, plus I had other jobs. I had lots of good friends and I helped a lot of people using my skills when they bought their houses, without charging them a penny!

We would work all night from Friday when they got the keys to their new house so that they could rent it out by Saturday. I wanted to buy a couple houses in the Hackney area because that's where the housing stock was at the time. But your mother left for America, so it would have been a struggle for me."

[Archer Publishing 2009]

But before my mother left, life was good…

"One good friend, Mr Pandit, lived one house away from us on Windsor Road and I helped him get the house inbetween. Pandit couldn't drive but he was a very successful insurance salesman, so I drove him in my car. And of course, I knew quite a lot of bus men and conductresses, and I was very popular with them - so I got sales with all types for him.

We went to lots of businesses selling insurance. In fact, Pandit became the top salesman of the year, beating people in the US, the Caribbean and Canada for 2 years in a row! He worked for a Canadian insurance company – so he did well when I was helping him. He even purchased a hotel with a casino on Tags Island in the East End where the Thames splits in two."

Mr Pandit and his wife were from Trinidad & Tobago. Mrs Pandit was very pretty and wore the most beautiful, colourful saris and gold bangles. I don't remember her speaking very much and I always felt that English was not her first language. But she was very kind to me.

I remember fun weekends spent with Mrs Pandit and her children up in the penthouse suite of their hotel after they'd moved from Windsor Road. The other adults would be downstairs in the hotel having fun – in bars and the casino I always thought - although dad has always maintained that he wasn't really into the gambling - and that a gambler can be worse than a thief.

So, we were all having fun and were one of the best dressed families in the area. I only wore expensive Clarks' shoes and top fashions from department stores like Harrods and Selfridges. And my brother always had the best too with money and packages being sent out to Jamaica for him, our cousins and my dad's younger brothers and sisters.

My father even regularly sent money out to his mother-in-law in Westmoreland (also in Jamaica), which I'm sure my grandmother ('Sita' - Syrian for Grandmother), was very grateful for because she was raising my mother's younger brothers on her own.

[Archer Publishing 2009]

But as some, including dad, often say: all good things must come to an end – and the good life was certainly coming to an abrupt end for Stanley Roy.

One of the red Route Master buses dad used to take me to work with him on to see all the top London sites - a fun activity which also helped to solve baby-sitting issues

PART III

"When Hortense left for America, she was supposed to be going to set up a good life for us all as a family. So I had to change from the buses to working on the school bus because I couldn't do the shifts. The officials at London Transport really tried to help me but it was still too difficult.

I used to do extra private plumbing jobs and moonlighting on the building to make ends meet. I used to have to carry you with me sometimes and ask the customers to let you sit and read and draw at their kitchen table. But you were well behaved so that wasn't a problem.

Anyway, I made good friends when I was on the school buses and I was very popular with all the staff and children. I used to get lovely steamed puddings and apple crumble from the cooks at the school to take home. I even used to see parents on behalf of the Headmaster and talk to them about their children. It was an SEN school."

[Archer Publishing 2009]

So, life took on a very different rhythm for Stanley Roy and his young daughter – and we quickly had to learn to dance to a new drum beat. Dad did everything for me from washing and combing my hair, which could be an all-day Saturday activity, to teaching me how to be safe at home as well as on the streets. But crucially, he also taught me how to be an independent little girl.

I remember hearing my dad mention the name 'Myra Hindley' (ref 10 page 185) * when being reminded not to talk to or go anywhere with strangers - or even take sweets from them. That woman's name always seemed to make me stop and think and it struck a note of fear within me. I didn't know any real details of who or what she'd done at the time – I was too young – but dad's method of using her name to teach me how to be safe, definitely worked.

It was when I started Grafton Primary School that I was presented with a navy blue ribbon with a copy of our front door key attached. I wore this around my neck under my vest (very cold in the winter) for years and was instructed in no uncertain terms that I should

<u>never</u> take it off! Whenever one of Aunt Ruby's daughters, Paulette or Jakki left the house with me, they would chant out in an attempt at a Jamaican accent: 'YUH HAVE YUH KEY?!' Of course, I always did and we'd always laugh.

In these times, I suspect that Children's Services might have taken me away as a child in need; the school might have informed them that at 7 years old, I was already a 'latch-door kid'. But although life was far from ideal for either of us, and dad worried about my safety hour to hour, I was loved.

The 1960s - feeding the pigeons in Trafalgar Square when it was still legal! Mrs Parish (my other mum along with Aunt Ruby) is between me (far right) **and Carol Malcolm. Mr Parish is far left and daughter Christine is 3rd from left.**

[Archer Publishing 2009]

(Shown in the previous photograph are Mr and Mrs Parish who were the caretakers of Grafton School when I attended. On the day the photograph was taken, they had taken a group of us from the area and the school out in their car for the day. Yes – cars were big! The Parishes were an integral part of our local community.)

As well as moonlighting, to help pay the mortgage on 55 Windsor Road, dad also took in lodgers. So apart from the bathroom, we were confined to the ground floor and garden of our 3-floor terraced house for some years. But Stanley Roy, being a man of many skills, had previously built an extension onto the back of our house in the garden – a sort of conservatory – and this gave us additional space as a playroom, a party room, a dining room and was a home for my piano for several years.

And in the summer, when the doors were always open
"Polly next door used to love your piano playing, especially the hymn" dad, proudly recalls.
Yes, we had some colourful neighbours! Polly, our lovely Welsh neighbour always seemed to be singing

our names in her accent and she loved to pop 'round to admire how beautifully dad kept the house. She wouldn't use the ashtrays she said, because they were too clean!

Polly couldn't start a new year without touching something black for luck. But very early in the morning on each January 1st, that 'thing' had to be my dad. As I grew up, this became offensive, but Polly was old and we knew she meant no harm. Bill, who she was married to, simply left her to it. He was an impressive and wise man who walked for miles each day well into his 80s; he'd run away to serve in the Great War of 1914, faking his age in the process.

'Milky', our local milkman, was another WWI vet. He was also married to a Welsh woman called Mary who ran the local diary at the corner of Windsor and Eburne Roads. The two couples were great friends and Dad was also a firm favourite with Mary for some reason. Adored by Milky, Mary died many years before him and he was never the same again. But later on, he seemed to find a new lease of life, despite being a widower, and Milky was honoured with a commission as a Beefeater at the Tower of London.

[Archer Publishing 2009]

So, good neighbours aside, financially, life was very difficult – 'stubborn' as dad liked to describe it. But we always ate the best food and being a farmer's son, dad managed to grow lots of fresh vegetables in our little garden.

My childhood friend, Carol Malcolm, also remembers that Stanley Roy had a seemingly insatiable appetite back in the day - despite him always being the same size throughout life. Carol remembers him telling her and her family how, when he used to work on the buses, he would stop at Smithfields Market, London's famous wholesale meat market, to buy his fresh Porter House steak.

I also remember that feather-bone steak was a regular on the Sunday morning breakfast menu along with freshly cut, steamed spinach from our back garden. And all these years later from Jamaica, Stanley Roy adds:

> *"I still love steak, but it's not good out here because the animals are too old!"*

Yes, he's certainly a 'matter-of-fact' man, as Carol likes to remind me!

And another of his black and white, matter-of-fact statements is about the value of a good education. So the financial hardships of life were not Stanley Roy's main concern. Somehow, he'd always manage and we wouldn't starve.

No, for Stanley Roy, his most important duty and main responsibility towards me was to ensure that my education was the very best I could get. So, he was there at every parents' meeting and as near to the front row as possible during every performance – smiling that smile!

> *"Oh yes, I was there at every open day, parents and teachers meetings, in fact, anything to do with the school that parents had to attend. I always had to be there. In fact, I got to know one or two of the teachers personally because you were so well behaved and loved at school. I never missed one school occasion – not one!"*

NOTES

* Myra Hindley, a convicted serial killer, was alsoknown as one of the Moors murderers, see also ref on page 176

[Archer Publishing 2009]

GLC/ILEA Wages

PAY NOTIFICATION

For codes see reverse

Tax Paid this yr £	Ni Code	Tax Code	Grade	Style	Name		Pay station	Pay Number
	PM	646	DR VR	MR	ARCHER STAN ROY		2062	E 01 2520

Additional Payment £	Additional Payment £	Additional Payment £	Additional Payment £	Additional Payment £		Basic Pay £ 22.95

Additional Payment £	Additional Payment £	Additional Payment £	Overtime £		Total Additions £

Deduction £	Deduction £	Deduction £	Deduction £		Gross Pay £ 22.95

Superann. Cons. £	Superann. Arrears £	Grad. Cons. £ 0.64	NI Deduct £ 0.88	Council's NI £ 0.95	Total Deductions £ 1.52

Tax Deduct £	NI Benefit Deduct. £	Amt. Subj. this week £	OT HOURS FIRST	x 1½	x 2	Net Pay £ 21.43

Other Deduction £		Reckonable Pay £ 136.80	Hrs. paid 40.00	Hourly/Wkly Rate £ 0.00 0.00 22.95	Wk No 06	Date 07 MAY

Taxable pay this week £ 22.95	Tax Pay this year £ 119.90

Stanley Roy's payslip for a week's wages for driving a school bus. Wages were paid by the **GLC ILEA** (Greater London Council, Inner London Education Authority)

Total: £22.95 gross, £21.43 net (after tax)

136

PART IV

Unlike most other parents from the Caribbean, Stanley Roy really came to understand how invaluable extracurricular activities could be for children. Although I wasn't allowed to play out on the street and as a result, never learned how to ride a bike, I had a very full social life outside school. Plus, I would soon learn how to side-steer a car and change its gears at a very early age!

Dad would patiently listen to my screeching violin as I practiced and never once asked me to stop the noise! The only practicing that he seemed to detest was my tap-dancing because he said the metal taps on my tap shoes scratched up the highly polished and well-maintained ceramic tiles in the kitchen!

[Archer Publishing 2009]

Another concert held in Grafton School: far left is Christine Parish and Yvonne; far right is Paulette (one of Aunt Ruby and Uncle Isby's six children)

Stanley Roy was a parent who believed in getting involved...

> *"I was a Committee Member at the Salterton Music Club* for many years. I went to all the meetings and was very active. We would go out to Sadler's Wells and the Royal Opera House and to recordings at the BBC where we weren't allowed to make __any__ noise. We couldn't even sneeze once they started the programme or eat a packet of crisps!*

I used to use my own car (a light blue Austin 1100) to ferry children to and from their parents after concerts, events and so on - and make sure they got home safely. I also transported stuff for jumble sales to raise funds for the club. And I remember Miss Amelia Percival (my blind piano teacher) knew me by my voice alone!"

Not surprising really dad, as you were the only committee member with a Jamaican accent!

"There was one other Black man on the committee for a short time. He was here with his wife and little son in London while he was studying. But then they went back to their country."

**Another Salterton Music birthday party held in the
main hall at Grafton School. Miss Percival is centre
cutting the cake with the then Mayor of Islington. Mr
Shires, her right-hand man, is standing far right.**
(I'm standing 3rd from left in the 2nd row)

Anyway, life trundled on during which time, I always heard dad whistling a couple of really melancholy tunes and hymns, and repeating the phrase *"life, oh life"*. He talked about going back home constantly - which wasn't surprising really as he didn't have any other family members around him.

It was 1972 - 18 years after he'd left Jamaica - before dad was finally able to return to visit his family.

> *"Everyone did long to see me, especially my mother. When I went back, I still called her 'Mama', taking up from where I'd left off before I went to England. But my brothers were calling her 'Mrs Archer' because they were grown."*

But despite a man of his age still calling his mother 'Mama', it wasn't long before everyone realised that here stood a man who was capable of doing anything and everything for himself <u>and</u> his daughter. He really didn't need his mother's or anyone else's help, although it was nice for him to be looked after for a change.

He remembers how one of girls who washed for the family had looked into his trunk that he'd travelled to Jamaica with and could only comment:

> *"Uh-um… how de underpants so white? Mi nuh tink sey me up to dis!"*

She really didn't think she was capable of keeping his underpants that clean and up to his standards of whiteness, so poor Roy lost his girl then and there!

[Archer Publishing 2009]

And out of the same trunk came another story:

> *"I had a lovely tracksuit – I don't know if you remember it? And Alecia** did take that. Mi nuh know how it fit her! She and her father and my nephew Roy came on the Sunday and I told them to look in the trunk and take <u>anything</u> they wanted."*

But once he was back in England, the trip home to Jamaica only seemed to make dad miss his brothers and sisters even more. He missed the good life with the sunshine and delicious fresh food and fruits; in fact, I don't know what he didn't miss! Don't get me wrong, lots of people talked about going 'back home' and some even explained that they'd only ever meant to stay in Britain for 5 or 10 years. But it seemed that dad was one of the few who really seemed to mean it.

Once I'd finished my education – that was it, according to dad! He would be making his arrangements to "*sell up and go back home*". And so said, so done! And again, to quote Carol Malcolm: "*He is a matter-of-fact man*!"

Stanley Roy Archer had originally planned to stay away from Jamaica for 20 years and was the only one amongst his circle of friends who actually went home before retirement. And with him, he took that same small, brown leather suitcase which he'd arrived with in London, way back in 1954.

Carol went on to give another example of how she and her family had come to the conclusion that Mr Archer is a matter-of-fact man…

"*In 1980, we were all at my nephew Anthony's christening party.*" The party took place at her mum's*** lovely flat which overlooks the River Lee in Hackney.

"*Aunt Zillah's grandson Brian was about 3 or 4 years of age at the time, and he stepped on Mr Archer's toe. So, Mr Archer ran him down and stepped on the little boy's toe and said: 'Go step pon yuh granny toe!'*"

Carol and her sister Sandra looked at each and tried not to burst out laughing! He was such a funny man. All they could do was to try to control their giggles. Even with children, Mr Archer was still a *"matter of fact man"*!

And this was a feature of Stanley Roy's character - although sometimes labelled as 'bluntness' – which was to prove invaluable. Along with his incredible qualities as a visionary and his energy, he was to go far and earn an untold amount of something that money can't buy when he finally got 'back home' - RESPECT.

"Up to last night, I had to tell them: Look, don't mention me when I get to a place. They have a way to say on the microphone on the music centre "Big up, Maas*** Roy, Big him up!" Even if I walk into the radio station, it's the same thing. Everybody in St Mary knows when I'm at the radio station.

Sometimes when you go for a drink or a meal, you don't want to be recognised; you just want to have a quiet time and be left alone. That's why I can understand how popular and famous people feel sometimes. Yes, I sympathise with them in a way.

When I go somewhere, everyone wants to see me. "Hey, Maas Roy, you know how long me want to see you, man. Maas Roy, I just want two minutes of

your time – beg yuh two minutes of your time, Sir' '
– they want to have a word with me! It can be a
damned pain in the rear when you're trying to go
somewhere or have a quiet drink! So what I tell
them is 'you know where I live' and 'I don't stop
them from coming up to the house.' "

And that's why my dad – 'Stanley Roy Archer', 'Mr Archer', 'Uncle Roy', 'Soldjie' or Maas Roy - has become loved and invaluable to the Jeffrey Town community and his family; everyone seems to believe that he has all the answers - and perhaps they're partially right!

NOTES

* The Salterton Music Club - England's first ever music centre was founded in 1958 by Miss Amelia Percival to offer lessons and playing to children and young people whose families otherwise could not afford it; she was awarded an MBE for her work. Club members include Jazzy Jeff and Coronation Street's 'Dev'.

** Alecia is Stanley Roy Archer's first grandchild by his son Ernel. He also has granddaughter Andrine and grandson Andre; he has 3 great-grandchildren.

*** Maas – Jamaican patois, an abbreviation for the title 'Master', although not in the sense of being someone junior in status, but rather a well skilled individual; the title is used as a sign of respect.

[Archer Publishing 2009]

CHAPTER THIRTEEN
"Community Leader and Activist"
Back on The Rock!

Stanley Roy Archer was someone who went home with the intention of fully re-integrating and engaging with his community as a 'returning resident'. He had no plans to live as though he was in Britain only in Jamaica and on a permanent Caribbean holiday, like many others. After all, why move to Jamaica if he wanted things to be like they were for him in London?

Anyway, when Stanley Roy finally arrived home in 1989, he found that very little had changed. This could have been great for a man who had dreamt of returning home for many years because the reality really did live up to the fond memories and he could easily have picked up where he'd left off.

But the reality could have been equally distressing for someone whose people hadn't seen any real progress since he'd left in 1954. Stanley Roy Archer was a man who had a revolutionary idea that would change life for the people of Jeffrey Town, St Mary for ever – especially its small farmers.

One day while they were sitting on his front verandah, Stanley Roy shared his vision of a farmer's co-operative with Jeffrey Town locals, Byron Gordon and Mr William - alias 'Muscler'. His idea was designed to help local farmers sell their produce more effectively.

> *"As individuals, local farmers couldn't supply their clients for long periods of time. For example, if they got an order from a hotel, they could only provide the amount of produce that the hotel needed for 2 or 3 weeks. But my idea was that if they planted and harvested at different times, the supply to the hotel would be more reliable and consistent and they would all be able to share the market.*
>
> *Well, I didn't know the local farmers at the time so Bryon Gordon and Muscler took the idea on the road to a local bar, and the idea spread like wild fire amongst the farmers!"*

[Archer Publishing 2009]

And thus, the Jeffrey Town Farmer's Co-operative was born - and people were grateful that 'Maas Roy', Jeffrey Town's own prodigal son, had decided to return home.

Meetings were soon held on Sunday evenings after church services at his brother Preshie's house, and each member had a vote. His old friend Lucien Bennett had also returned to live in Jamaica with his family from Birmingham in England, and he became one of the founding members along with his brother, Maas Barry.

The main aim of the Co-operative was to find ways of bringing an income into the homes of the people of Jeffrey Town. The Co-operative would thus empower them, raise their self-esteem and encourage the aspirations of the community's young people, delivering free training whenever possible. Like the Right Excellent Marcus Garvey [1], Stanley Roy Archer believed that if people could unite, success could be enjoyed by all.

But first, there was one thing that needed Stanley Roy's urgent attention. It was heart-rending for him to encounter because it had been the same since he was a boy. This 'thing' forced him to follow a path which meant that his life back on The Rock [2] would be no easy ride; he wouldn't be due for early retirement after all.

The sight of little children struggling long distances to collect clean water, which they'd carry on their little heads for miles, like he used to, to wash and cook breakfast - even before going to school - was too much for Stanley Roy to witness. How could this <u>still</u> be happening in a modern world?

In his day, the Archer children were lucky in a way because they could take a short cut to the clean water supply - and there's a history to that, as Stanley Roy heard it told:

> *"The Headmanship [3] for that land was in the Marsh family and it had always been that way. But one of the Marshes was a drunkard.*

[Archer Publishing 2009]

One night, he was stone drunk and fell off his horse in a dark place. Apparently, my father was coming from St Ann's [4] in the dark and frightened Marsh. The horse had found his way home earlier and when Marsh's wife saw the horse without her husband, she was frightened and everyone was out looking for him. But my father drew a match and stumbled along with the man until he managed to get him home.

From that time on, the Marsh family were very grateful to my father and anything that we children wanted from that land was available to us. We shot and roasted birds and took firewood. There's no other reason that I can think of why we Archer children were so privileged.

We could take our cows to Spring Gardens to graze… we could help ourselves to coconuts, pimento, lime – anything! And my father was given a piece of land to work for himself.

When I was small, I dreamt of buying this piece of land for my father (Spring Gardens). It was selling in

1972, but due to marital problems, I was unable to buy it. I still got part of it anyway, so I suppose I fulfilled part of my ambition.

But prior to that, when I was small, all children in the area had to take their buckets of water to and from the road via the right hand side of the land - and they had try to pass the Headman (Marsh) *and dash like thief under the wire!*

When children were coming back up the hill with buckets on their heads, they couldn't see him because their vision was restricted and if they tried to look up or move their heads, the water would be spilled and they would get wet. And if he saw them, he would cut off their journey and they might get turned back with the water. But after my father saved the Headman, the Archer children were allowed to cut through to collect their water.

In 1991, we (the Co-op) *got a young Public Health Inspector, someone from the United Nations and an Environmental Engineer from the US to inspect all 11 water holes in the area - and only 1 was approved for domestic use. All the others were condemned."*

Stanley Roy had returned to Jamaica decades later, only to learn the distressing news that clean water in Jeffrey Town was even scarcer than it was when he was a child!

"There was no water and that put us into action! They said that the water holes were unsuitable for domestic use and human consumption and dumped marl[5] into them. But I said they <u>must</u> offer an alternative source of water or explain to people why the water holes were closed. We were the only organisation that was recognised as doing anything of social use in the area."

Stanley Roy and the founding members tried to negotiate and work with the Jamaican Water Commission without success, so eventually...

"With the help of the then local councillor, Bobby Montague, we applied for and won funding from the United Nation's Development Programmes (UNDP) through the Jamaican 'Life Programme'. But the UNDP would only provide funding for two pumps to

pump water from the water source three miles
away. So the MP at the time, Terrence Gillett, then
came aboard and provided the pipes we needed.
But there was no funding provided for labour."

So again, Stanley Roy rallied the troops and led the revolution, getting volunteers to help him prepare the land for running and embedding the 3 miles of water pipes through the area. The newly run pipes would allow locals to access clean, running water from taps along the road for the first time in years. And if they wanted and were able to, they could then run pipes into their homes.

The provision of clean running water was something that the Jamaican Water Commission had somehow been incapable of accomplishing for several years. The reasons why were never made clear.

I remember visiting Jeffrey Town a few times before my dad had returned home and having access to clean running water once every 3 days. This had become accepted as the norm by people living there – and 'what can we do?' became a response to my questions. So the very first project for the Jeffrey Town Farmer's

Association became The Water Project - and as a result, Maas Roy was deservedly awarded the St Mary's National Heroes Day Award for service in the field of community service!

Being formally recognised as a local hero only seemed to provide Maas Roy with more steam and he went on to use the same formula of recruiting volunteers and uniting people for the good of the community. Next came the Dairy Project...

"As the Jeffrey Town Farmers' Association (JTFA), we tried to rekindle our relationship with the Nestles condensary [6] as a means of bringing an income into the homes of the small farmers. The condensary market still existed. So working with Nestles' condensary, farmers worked together to provide fresh milk for the factory.

The initial idea was to obtain milking cows and the Association was given money by its local MP at the time to start them off by buying cows. JFTA also aligned itself with the agricultural side of Nestles to get support. We got the fresh milk truck running

*every morning to pick up the milk and their sales
provided a form of income for local people.*

*This proved helpful until a foreign source flooded
the market with a lot of cheap diary products and
powdered milk - which completely spoiled the
market for the Jeffrey Town farmers and the whole
island. So that died a death.*"

Next, the unstoppable Maas Roy started thinking about
the lack of medical provision for local people. The co-
operative took on the responsibility of repairing and
maintaining a shack shelter made of plywood with a
corrugated iron roof and they would regularly clear the
small medical clinic's yard of weeds. But later, he
managed to install a flushing toilet at his own expense
because he felt it totally unfair for pregnant women in the
area, who didn't have the ability to travel to other more
well-equipped clinics, to have to use an old pit toilet [7].

Now, Jeffrey Town even has a social club which
acknowledges and celebrates things from members'
birthdays to local heroes such as a long-serving
community midwife, Nurse Gordon. And despite being

well past retirement age, the energetic Stanley Roy Archer continues to work actively in his community to make further improvements to the area. And the gloves are off!

"*We're going to put Jeffrey Town on the map and give everyone a sense of ownership and pride in the area!*" he declares.

Some years ago, dad was integral in getting the very first payphones installed in Jeffrey Town and is still working on getting landline service to it as access to the internet becomes increasingly desirable and useful for people in the area.

Maas Roy even attempted to start a neighbourhood watch scheme some years ago, and even though this didn't quite pan out on a formal basis, his work has seen some success. As a result of increased community cohesion, there's now less criminal activity in the area making it a safer neighbourhood for all.

Several other farming-based projects have also been started under the Association's umbrella since its formation in 1991. The Co-op became an Association and has been registered along the way and its projects have lead to some wonderful successes. These include:

- ✓ The annual Breadfruit Festival [8] which has been sponsored by the Jamaican Tourist Board and the Jamaica National Building Society amongst others
- ✓ The banana, poultry, goat, cassava and pepper projects which were sponsored by the European Union
- ✓ The upgraded Grade 1 Health Centre sponsored by Digicell and Chase Fund
- ✓ The community radio station, JET 88.7 FM which was sponsored by UNESCO
- ✓ The Multi-Media Centre with help from Jamaica's Ministry of Technology & Communication
- ✓ The literacy project with help from Jamaica's Life-Long Learning Programme
- ✓ AND MUCH MORE!!

Of late, the young people of Jeffrey Town have been consulting my dad on the formation of a youth club! Of course, dad is happy to oblige as a consultant and draws on his experiences of being a dedicated committee member of the Salterton Music Club in London back in the day. The only payment he asks is that the youth club will serve a more useful role than simply being somewhere for youths to 'idle' – waste time, e.g. educational and cultural elements to the club's activities would be most appreciated.

During dad's updates on the progress of the Jeffrey Town Youth Club, I often wonder whether the young people realise that dad's actually in his late 70s?! But it seems that he may be the only elder in the area who the local youths feel able to engage with, trust and confide in - and have the ability and will to do something about helping them achieve their dreams.

Based on the way my own friends have always related to my dad, I can say with certainty that he definitely has a concrete understanding of and concern for young people's needs. So could it be that Maas Roy is one of the world's oldest youth workers?!

So there we have it – "*Life According to Maas Roy*"! And each time we get down to work on the phone, I'm treated to a few more stories or an update - but always a serious joke or two with <u>my dad</u>.

So, we hope these memoirs will inspire, educate and amuse you as much as they have us - and that they'll also lead you to think about and openly debate the topics we've covered. May you also become a leader in your own right, rather than waiting for others to be the ones to make a real difference to your family, community, country – or at the very least, within yourself.

> "*As we say in Jamaica, no man is an island by himself. You're not alone – you'll always have another island beside you!*"

**Let's all try to be the best we can be -
and always remember
that without each other,
we are nothing.
UBUNTU!** [9]

NOTES FROM CHAPTER 13

[1] Marcus Garvey was one of Jamaica's first National Heroes.

[2] The Island of Jamaica is often called 'The Rock' in fondness.

[3] The Headman of an estate was like a foreman who acted on behalf of the land owner.

[4] St Ann's – a parish which neighbours St Mary.

[5] Marl is a type of stone often used for filling holes in the roads

[6] Condensary – a factory where sweetened condensed milk is made and canned.

[7] A basic toilet made by digging a very deep hole in the ground , approximately 6- 8 feet deep and packed around with stone from the ground up. A toilet bowl and seat are placed on them but there is no flushing water.

[8] Breadfruit is the large green fruit of a tree which is cooked and eaten like a staple, such as rice; it was first imported from the Pacific islands in 1793 to feed enslaved African peoples in Jamaica. The last festival was in July 2009 after a 2 year hiatus due to sponsorship issues.

[9] Ubuntu is a Southern African word which is difficult to define but easy to understand if we think of how Maas Roy lives his life, e.g. I can only be the best I can be if I help you to also be the best you can be.

Stanley Roy's son, Ernel (Len) who was born 12th June 1952

**Above, a penny dated 1916;
Below, a ha'penny dated 1947
(larger than the actual size).
Both were saved by Stanley
Roy through the years and
represent ½ the bus fare he had
to pay to get to his very first job
in England.**

The GSM (General Service Medal) Gunner Archer was awarded in 1959. Back then, the GSM was awarded for any type of duty whether it was active or not.

The back of
Gunner Archer's
medal

Yvonne's 5th birthday photograph

Yvonne at Grafton Infants School approx aged 6 - reading as usual!

Aunt Ruby (a mum to Yvonne) at her surprise 70th birthday party!

Maas Roy and Yvonne on his 75th birthday; Mahogany Beach, Jamaica
(Photo courtesy of Yuko Maeda 2007,
Photoshop by William Kremer)

Maas Roy - the world's oldest youth worker?

Photo courtesy Yuko Maeda 2007

Formally recognised as a local hero, Maas Roy is presented with an award at a formal international event by a local teacher (27th December 2008)

SIGNIFICANT DATES AND FURTHER INFO

Date		Significant Dates and Further Info
1838	The official abolition of slavery	Many former slave owners went on to become employers of formerly enslaved people.
1887 – 1940	The Right Excellent Marcus Mosiah Garvey Jr was one of Jamaica's first National Heroes	Stanley Roy believes this man was "*one of the world's biggest brains - Black or White*" - an international leader who did a lot of inspired work in the US. Stanley Roy had heard about him early on in life but only got details much later on of how this man organised and united Black people. He learned what this Black man stood for and believes that everything he forecast has actually come to pass. In Stanley Roy's opinion, this most courageous of men was jailed by the Governor of Jamaica because Jamaican rulers were afraid of him and the power he had over the people of Jamaica. Stanley Roy remains amazed that a Black man as far back as 1914 could organise the buying of the Black Star Line shipping company to enable people of African heritage to return to the African continent.
30th March 1932	Stanley Roy Archer was born in St Ann, Jamaica at home	In those days, children's births weren't registered as soon as they were born. Often, relatives or neighbours would be sent to the nearest Post Office which registered births and deaths.

[Archer Publishing 2009]

AND 31st January 1932	Leaving them to do the job obviously lead to many incorrect dates and spelling of names being registered. This remains an issue across Jamaica today. Stanley Roy's actual date of birth is 31st January 1932 and he was one of 11 children, although not all sharing the same parents.
24th May 1938 General Strike in Jamaica while Britain celebrated Empire Day	Stanley Roy still has vivid memories of soldiers driving through Jeffrey Town in an attempt to flush out the young men who had joined in the strike which brought Jamaica and the Jamaican sugar industry to its knees. Young local men hid in the bushes. He knew, even as a boy, that this was a particularly dangerous time.
1944 General Adult suffrage	Jamaica was the 1st British Colony to be granted adult suffrage. Originally, only people over 21 could vote. Much later on, voting rights were granted to over 18s. Stanley Roy realised the importance of adult literacy at a very early age. Pre-1944, "*if a man couldn't read and write and owned enough land and paid taxes there was no space for him*" – in terms of the ballot box and society. This helped Stanley Roy form the very firm opinion that owning your own land in Jamaica is important and later on, the view that farming and being able to feed yourself and the nation is much more of a priority than tourism in Jamaica. In official circles, tourism is prioritised over farming - which he strongly objects to.

		Incidentally, 1944 was also the year of a particularly *"bad hurricane which flattened Western St Mary. It was on a Sunday!"*
14th December 1944	General Election	The 1st held in Jamaica under Adult Suffrage. Stanley Roy was of course, too young to vote and had left for England before Jamaica became independent. His 1st vote as an adult would be in England.
12th June 1952	Birth of son, Ernel Archer	'Len', or 'Ringo' as he's known, was taken from the verandah of his mother's house by his paternal grandfather, Jeremiah Archer. At only a few months old, his grandfather felt the Archers were more capable of caring for him. Along with several cousins, Len was raised by Stanley Roy and family within the Archer household - deemed to be a good environment for all Archers. His Dad remembers how he loved cooked green bananas.
Winter of 1954	Arrived in England	Stanley Roy left Jamaica on the 13th October, travelling for 6 weeks by sea aboard the MV Napoli - an Italian refloated war ship fitted with dormitories and bunk beds. *"I loved the sea. I loved to look at the waves and the big, big fish in the sea."*

[Archer Publishing 2009]

1956 – 1959	National Service	Gunner Archer served on active duty during the conflict in Cyprus. He has a GSM (General Service Medal) to show for it, given to all who did national service, whether active duty was served or not.
1959	Death of Jeremiah Nathaniel Archer	His father who died just after he'd returned from Cyprus; he was waiting to be demobbed so that he could return to London.
1960	Marriage to Hortense Wright	A teacher in Jamaica, she worked as his bus conductress in London when he drove trolley buses. It was an ill-fated and short-lived marriage.
27th May 1961	Birth of daughter, Yvonne Archer	He took on overall responsibility for his daughter as soon as she left the hospital and by about 1965, was raising her alone in London after his wife left for the US. One summer, the Archers in Jamaica were to discuss keeping his 6-year old daughter who'd been visiting from London because she "had no mother".
1962	Jamaican independence	Although still part of the Commonwealth, Jamaica was no longer under British rule and could elect its own Prime Minister. Stanley Roy was not there to vote.

1963	Bought a house in London for £4,500	The house was 55 Windsor Road in Holloway (in the London Borough of Islington). He chose the area because he'd lived in and around the area for many years, he had good friends there and it had good transport links and shops etc.
Christmas 1972	First trip back home to Jamaica	18 years after he'd left, he'd finally saved enough money to visit his mother back home.
29th December 1979	Death of Desmond Archer in Canada	With the passing of his brother 'Uncle D', Stanley Roy took on the mantle of 'Senior Archer'.
1982	Marriage to Anceline Spence – his 2nd marriage	Another doomed marriage for Stanley Roy that ended very acrimoniously but toughened him up, helping him to acknowledge and prepare for his pending role as a leader amongst family, community and within the land of his birth.
13th April 1984	Death of Elmore Archer (nee Higgins)	Born in 1900, Sir Roy's beloved 'Mama' died peacefully and without any real health issues apart from senile dementia or possibly mild Alzheimer's. Luckily, Stanley Roy had been visiting her in Jamaica at the time so he was still there when she passed away.

[Archer Publishing 2009]

1989	Stanley Roy returned home to Jamaica 'for good'.	He had bought and was renovating and extending a little stone house in Spring Gardens which had a spring nearby. His father had worked on that land whilst the days of slavery were not such a distant memory and Stanley Roy had always promised himself that he'd buy it for his father some day. He remembers how the land produced the sweetest and best fruits available and only the Archer children were privileged enough to walk through that piece of land to fetch clean water, collect fruits and hunt birds with their sling shots for roasting. Spring Gardens is still regarded as the most desirable and admired property in Jeffrey Town to date.
1991	Founding of the Jeffrey Town Farmers' Co-operative	He shared his vision of a farmer's co-operative with locals Byron Gordon and Mr William alias 'Muscler'. Maas Barry and brother Lucien Bennett, also a returning resident from England, soon became founding members. It's now registered as the Jeffrey Town Farmers' Association Ltd (JFTA Ltd).
1991 onwards	Jeffrey Town Farmers' Association Ltd started several projects including:	Many smaller projects were formed under the umbrella of the Co-operative, and later on the Association, to help locals meet market needs and provide a form of income for people with no other means of earning a living. The only thing they had of value was land. Most of the resources to get the Association up and running came from Stanley Roy's own pockets, e.g. use of his personal telephone (causing bitter arguments within his marriage) and after a while, meetings took place at his home.

The Diary Project	When Stanley Roy was little, the Nestles Condensary (where condensed milk was made and canned) was built to take milk from the small farmers, providing them with a fortnightly income. The Association tried to rekindle this source of income for people in Jeffrey Town but success was short-lived as cheaper diary products from a foreign source flooded the market.
The Banana and Cassava Project, The Medical Clinic Project (providing water supply for the toilet)	Requirements for the foreign market were so costly that the farmers were unable to continue growing bananas for sale without making a loss. The Cassava project aimed to provide produce for the chip factory but vital support from government officials following the research and pilot projects were not as forthcoming as had been hoped. As a result, the cassava project was discontinued.
The Poultry, Goat, Pig, Cassava Projects,	The Poultry Project didn't last because cheaper chicken meat was being imported from the US, making it difficult for local farmers to sell their own produce and compete in the market.
The Pepper Project	With Jamaica's hottest 'scotch bonnet' and ''Jamaica red' peppers being vital ingredients in the famous 'Walkers Wood' brand of jerk seasoning, this remains an open market for members of the JTFA Ltd. They have guaranteed sales for any peppers they manage to grow, no matter the size or shape.

[Archer Publishing 2009]

	The Rabbit Project	Unfortunately, this project is still struggling to get off the ground due to unpredictable amounts of rain and erratic seasons – a very real result of Global Warming, affecting the livelihood of small, struggling farmers. With the discovery that rabbits are easy to raise, low in cholesterol, high in protein and hormone free because of what they're fed – plus the fact that a single jerk rabbit leg can command a price of $1,000 Jamaican dollars (approx £6.00), Stanley Roy had envisioned this would be an easy source of income for Jeffrey Town's single mothers, enabling them to send their children to school. Many children in Jeffrey Town don't attend school regularly because their parents don't have enough money for uniforms, shoes and other materials. The droppings of the rabbits were also found to be a natural pesticide and fertilizer, taking farming in Jeffrey Town a little closer to organic methods.
16th October 2000	Stanley Roy Archer was awarded the St Mary's National Heroes Day Award for service in the field of Community Service	With this award came the official realisation for all that Stanley Roy Archer is a living local hero and role model!

176

April 2002	Stanley Roy was awarded 1st prize at the St Mary Agricultural Show for Eastern Jamaica	The award was given by RADA (Royal Agricultural Development Agency) and the Jamaican Agricultural Society. Stanley Roy's cross-breed of a South African goat with the common Jamaican breed led to a much more intelligent and faster growing animal. Subsequent versions of this new cross-breed are to be found across the parish of St Mary and the Jeffrey Town Goat Breeders' Association is on the map!
		This was the first time that doctors, dentists, opticians and other medical specialists from the US and Canada came to Jeffrey Town. The team of medical staff was made up of volunteers, and teams have made several additional trips since. They offer free medical examinations and check-ups, some medication plus information on where free prescription glasses can be obtained.
2005	RADA donated a vehicle for community use	The Royal Agricultural Development Association provided a vehicle, to be used for the development of the community's projects – particularly agricultural development.

[Archer Publishing 2009]

2006	Winning of the Michael Manley Foundation Award for Community Self-Reliance for the Jeffrey Town Farmers' Association Ltd	Unfortunately, due to the unplanned seating arrangements in the theatre, Stanley Roy and the other founding members didn't manage to get to the award before the press took their photos! Stanley Roy is a little photo shy anyway and tends to avoid the limelight as he's *"more interested in getting things done for the community"*.
August 2006	The 1st Jeffrey Town Annual Breadfruit Festival	The festival takes place around Emancipation Day as Stanley Roy believes it is of greater significance than Jamaica's Independence Day. A huge success, the festival placed a welcome spotlight on the community where innovative and inspirational things were happening - thanks to Stanley Roy's vision. He chose the humble but highly versatile breadfruit as it is an important food to the history of Jamaica. Following near famine after a series of severe hurricanes, the breadfruit was imported in 1793 from the Pacific Islands to help feed Jamaica's enslaved people. Due to a downturn in the global economy, there was no festival in 2008 but popular demand and promises of sponsorship forced its return on Sunday July 19th 2009.
2007	Jeffrey Town Farmers' Association Multi-Media Centre, mainly funded by UNESCO	Work started on building a Multi-Media Centre on land donated by the Burrell family and Jeffrey Town's first computers arrived. The centre was set up to help increase literacy amongst adults in the community, aid learning for children and to disseminate useful information to local farmers, amongst other things. For many locals, this provided their first ever experience of a computer and shortly after, the internet.

Date		
		The Multi-Media centre was developed and run with the aid of a US Peace Corps volunteer, Albert Little. One of his main objectives in coming to Jamaica was to pass on basic computer skills to enable people to apply for jobs and increase efficiency within businesses across the island. After 2 years of service and living and working in the Jeffrey Town community, Albert was sad to return home to the US.
27th May 2008	Launch of JET FM 88.7, Local Community Radio Station	Run by the Jeffrey Town Farmers' Association, the aim is to provide information on farming practices, empower members of the community, raise self-esteem and aspirations amongst young people and be a source of media training which has already lead to other vocational courses and job opportunities for some. Stanley Roy and daughter Yvonne were involved in the initial planning and motivational stages in terms of conveying the vision, brainstorming programming ideas and identifying training needs.
27th December 2008	Stanley Roy Archer received a Jeffrey Town Education Association award for his outstanding service to the community	A big event which was well attended and included several guests from Canada and America who were present for their Jeffrey Town Past Students' Association reunion.

[Archer Publishing 2009]

| 1st April 2009 | Official ground-breaking for the new Jeffrey Town Health Centre | Co-ordinated by Stanley Roy, his vision was to provide dignity and hygienic facilities for people utilising local health services, particularly as the old clinic was used mainly by pregnant women and babies who are largely unable to travel long distances to get to the nearest medical centres. Utilising his plumbing and building skills and personal money, he'd previously financed and installed a flushing toilet at the former clinic. He hopes to acquire an ambulance in the future.

This project, as with all others, relies on Stanley Roy's charm, leadership qualities, skills, experience, vision, honesty and instincts to

➤ recruit, inspire and retain volunteers from the community
➤ liaise with sponsors and officials
➤ mediate during disputes. |

AFTERNOTE:

These memoirs form part of the first phase of our project entitled "**Our Peace of History**" – a project which aims to help further the cause of peace and understanding amongst various people and across generations. I began serious work on it following the British Council's "Trust the Difference" peace and understanding programme.

We are encouraging and working with other people of African heritage to also find their own way of telling their stories to help highlight the importance of our role in and contribution to British society. Dad and I have already begun to bridge 'the generation gap' by working together on these memoirs and look forward to the positive benefits that young people and their elders will also no doubt gain by working together on films, plays, poetry, music, photography, dance, etc.

We <u>know</u> that Black people in Britain have important stories to tell and so we're saying it again: it's obvious that <u>we</u> are the people who must tell those stories. Without our contributions, British history is incomplete, sketchy and inaccurate at best.

[Archer Publishing 2009]

We now ask that you carefully consider and truthfully answer the following question:

There are other local Black heroes out there whose shoulders we stand on to reach the top – but only for a limited time. Is it right for such phenomenal people to be invisible within British history?

Please contact us for help and/or ideas on how to unlock and document the stories you hold from our shared history. But beware – you'll then become a part of an exciting and historic project in the making!!

For more information or to give comments and feedback on this book or on our project:
email **ourpeaceofhistory@gmail.com**

Also, visit our website at **www.ourpeaceofhistory.com** for information on collaborative opportunities for teachers, invitations to and details on upcoming readings, workshops, events plus ideas on how individuals can get involved.

These memoirs will also be available in other formats at a later date, such as an audio and workbooks to make them accessible and useful to as many people as possible across the generations. Again, please check our website for details and send us your requests and ideas via e-mail.

We dedicate our publication to the youths of Britain and the youths of our global village with love and in the hope that:

- ✓ it inspires and imparts knowledge and understanding
- ✓ it establishes a path to a firm grounding in basic values and morals
- ✓ it helps develop respect for self, elders and community
- ✓ it awakens us all to the idea that <u>everyone</u> can dream and make those dreams come true

Our visions for tomorrow
are valid and valued!

[Archer Publishing 2009]

BIBLIOGRAPHY / REFERENCES / ADDITIONAL INFORMATION

[1] *House of Commons sittings:*

31st January 1956:

http://hansard.millbanksystems.com/commons/1956/jan/31/cyprus-national-service-men

3rd July 1956:

http://hansard.millbanksystems.com/commons/1956/jul/03/national-service-men-cyprus

[2] *Information courtesy of The British Cyprus Memorial Trust, as compiled by David Carter:*

To view the roll call:

http://www.britishcyprusmemorial.org/index.php/roll

Planned memorial, as organised and reported by David Carter:

http://www.britishcyprusmemorial.org/index.php/about

[3] *Kelso Cochrane*

http://news.bbc.co.uk/1/hi/programmes/4871898.stm

[4] *Claudia Jones*

http://en.wikipedia.org/wiki/Claudia_Jones

[5] *Background to the link between the Cyprus Emergency and WWI:*

http://en.wikipedia.org/wiki/EOKA

[6] *Information on EOKA, as compiled by David Carter:*

http://www.britains-smallwars.com/cyprus/Most%20wanted/most_wanted.html

[7] *George Grivos, courtesy of David Carter:*

http://www.britains-smallwars.com/cyprus/Most%20wanted/most_wanted.html

[8] *BBC News from 1956 on Archbishop Makarios:*

http://news.bbc.co.uk/onthisday/hi/dates/stories/march/10/new sid_4216000/4216931.stm

[9] *BBC News re: Mau Maus legal action against the British*

http://news.bbc.co.uk/1/hi/uk/6042524.stm

[10] *BBC News – Obituary on Myra Hindley*

http://news.bbc.co.uk/1/hi/england/452614.stm

National Library of Jamaica

http://www.nlj.org.jm/civics.htm

The Right Excellent Marcus Mosiah Garvey, Jamaican National Hero

http://www.bbc.co.uk/history/historic_figures/garvey_marcus.s html

Google Map showing location of Jeffrey Town

http://www.maplandia.com/jamaica/saint-mary/jeffrey-town/

Official recognition for the Jeffrey Town Farmer's Association

http://www.jamaica-gleaner.com/gleaner/20060813/focus/focus4.html

History of the Breadfruit in Jamaica

http://www.jamaica-gleaner.com/pages/history/story0019.html

Launch of JET 88.7 FM goes on air (correction, Ivy Gordon is the JTFA's Secretary) – Stanley Roy Archer is shown in a blue shirt, centre back

http://portal.unesco.org/ci/en/ev.php-URL_ID=26824&URL_DO=DO_PRINTPAGE&URL_SECTION=201.html